Life Through The Eyes Of A Smile

Calvin Simpson

Adele, I wish you
the happiest & most
successful life through the
eyes of a smile!

Take this book and spread it around as you please.

As you read jump in on the conversation by sharing your thoughts to social media with the corresponding chapter #'s.
Twitter - @eyesofasmile
Instagram - @eyesofasmile
Facebook - https://www.facebook.com/CalvinSimpsonSmile

Want to turn your blog into a book?
Calvin@happful.com
www.happful.com

10% of the proceeds of this book will be donated annually to the Stollery Childrens Hospital

Life Through The Eyes Of A Smile/ Calvin Simpson. —1st ed.
ISBN 978-0-9950905-0-7

Contents

Dedication to my wonderful family Vangi, Eugene, Clayton and Jody

A special thank you to Melissa Smith, without your help this book would still be in my head

An extended thank you to all those wonderful individuals who have supported me through my LinkedIn writing – Angela Lemme, Benjamin Klein, Brandon Mahowich, David Burrowes, David Hatch, Denise McDowell, Dennis Sedurifa, Dr. Khairil Osman, Elizabeth Lyon, Fareed Ebrahim, Gerson Silva, Jamie Young, Jared Laird, Jeffrey Strickland, Jim Ryan, John Musgrove, John Ryan, Josip Lovric, Karl Hodtwalker, Khalid Ansari, Mario Luces, Martin Wright, Mauro Jagle, Michael Dahlseide, Michele Knight, Mohamed Wasim, Nan Xi, Nick Watson, Polina Arapov, Raja Sengupta, Rene Goudreau, Robert Orlak, Robert San Miguel, Ronjit Mukherjee, Ryan Dalmer, Salma Rodriguez, Salman Mahmood, Sarah Elkins, Saudah Chan, Swapnil Ghorpade, Tammy Trippler, Trevor Textor, Trevor Valan, Yumiko Sun

Introduction

After graduating college in 2010, I had the world ahead of me, a ton of ambition and the interests of a 20-year-old. No job currently locked down, but many detailed cover letters and custom resumes left me excited for the coming career and kick-off to a life of perfecting my craft and enjoying the high wages and joy that would surely come from them. My long weekend was coming, and it was time to continue the graduation celebration—not that we needed an excuse at 20. A group of seemingly strong bonded boys gathered to drink and party like only 20-year-olds know how to. A long night of partying ensued before each straggler returned back to the central house. Showing up last and also cashless, I needed support to pay the cab driver for his efforts. Into the house I went, and a joyful new acquaintance met me with a smile and the money I needed to pay the man for his efforts.

Outside, we reminisced about the night's tales after splitting up early on. The cab driver was paid and as he drove away, a group of individuals walked onto the lawn, greeting us with a tense approach and threatening words. These individuals were new to me but familiar to my new cab-paying buddy. Earlier in the night, a bar altercation turned violent, and both parties were kicked out of the bar. Unbeknownst to my new friend or me, they were not ready to end their fight. They waited outside of the house until the opportune moment arose for the fight to continue. As we traded words, one of the men on the other side came from behind, wielding a bat. After fleeing for surely his life, my new friend disappeared while I was continually struck. I came to in the hospital, hours later, surrounded by family.

"Why am I here? What happened?" were questions that repeated as I came in and out of consciousness. The confusing yet soon-to-be very sobering responses began to weigh on me as surgeon after surgeon turned away the case due to complexity.

A surgeon took the phone call in the morning and thankfully agreed to the task at hand. This man was Dr. Gorman Louie, a plastic surgeon specializing in craniofacial surgery at the University of Alberta Hospital. Dr. Louie was truly a man doing amazing things in his life to help others. An initial surgery of around eight hours brought my broken and shattered jaw into place for recovery. Two days later, doctors discovered a displaced fracture in my arm and a broken hand, which were repaired in an intense surgery while I was awake.

Plates, screws and scars reminded me of this time everyday, as well as provided the mark of this reminder for life. In total I spent seven days in the hospital with what were considered to be fairly serious injuries for the ward. Looking back now, the experience would have been considered a drop of water in a lake for many in the hospital, primarily in the ward I drove most inspiration from. The adult ward I was in was nearly void of any positive emotion. There were a few laughs to be had, but it did not take long for them to be enveloped by the energy vacuum being transmitted by the in-patients. The best part of my day occurred when I was up for walks around the hospital. On my floor was a bright and energetic ward, one that was much different than any other place in the hospital. This spot was the waiting area for the Stollery Children's Hospital. My stay was most dearly remembered for the uplifting time spent walking through this section of the hospital.

A question still burned in my head: why are we as adults so easily sucked into drains of self-pity and worry over situations that do not deserve the attention? The children in this ward had all the right in the world to be down and upset over their situations; however, they did not subscribe to this "woe is me" attitude. Many were still able to find smiles in their days, pushing forward with drive and determination to pull the best out of every day.

After this experience, I have been much more attuned to how people handle themselves under their given circumstances. How could so very many of these kids, all with very serious ailments, be capable of such admirable joy? How could an individual walking down the street have a day ruined by a stubbed toe or by stepping into a puddle? There are so many sayings out there that help inspire us: Happiness is yours if you so choose. Life is full of choices, and I choose happiness. Happiness depends on us. I have looked for happiness to grab out of the air, on the shelves at stores and in anyone that I could find around me. I couldn't find it in the air, anywhere in a store (not even in the discount bins), and it was not on my to-do list for the year.

There is this great word that floats around in the air as the key to unlocking our happiness. If we can just get this then everything else will work itself out, including a life with more smiles. It seems to be tied to cars, houses, and pleasures in the news. This word is "success". What does success mean to you?

4

This is not an automatic answer; think deep on this one. Think career success, relationship success, leaving a legacy of success. There is no easy pill to success. You will not wake up one day and think, "Well I have this thing called success now, what is next?" I look at success as being a direct product of happiness and fulfillment. These two are very closely tied together, the way a cat's reaction to being happy is to purr. Our reaction to happiness and fulfillment is a true smile, one that comes not only from the lips, but the eyes as well. This true, not falsely constructed form of a smile, is called the Duchenne smile, first discovered in the 1800s (talk about blast from the past). This version of a smile is very hard to fake for most people (barring a few actors) and can be identified by contracting muscles around the eyes. Can you tell when someone is just putting a fake smile on?

For the purposes of this book, the word happiness will be defined as the result of any experiences in our life that bring true smiles to our faces. Success in life is determined by the quantity and quality of smiles we experience and leave behind over a lifetime. Success shall not be no longer be defined as what we find before our happiness. It comes after.

This is not just a book on telling you to live a happier life, filled with those familiar clichés about happiness. I think these types of quotes are great but tend to leave people with blind hope, often not improving happiness in life at all. These statements actually create more confusion out of missed expectations, which ultimately leads to a life with fewer smiles. To think that every day will be nothing but peachy and awesome is completely absurd. You will not wake up with a smile every single day and tap dance through your day, ending with a smile smacking the pillow.

My goal in writing this book, rather, is to provide you with new tools to actively add smiles to your day and to others' days. We have the opportunity to have a genuine smile once a day if we simply become more aware of the small things that trigger those grins. Dan Gilbert fully dissects the word "happiness" in his book, Stumbling on Happiness. He approaches the topic from an insightful, laboratory-based approach. What we can learn from his research and his dissection of happiness is that it is not the same for all of us. Happiness is subjective. Who are we to tell a 12-year-old that cake will not be the thing that provides us ultimate happiness in life, when it does at that very time? I find elevated levels of happiness when riding a scooter along the coastline in a foreign country when I am exploring. This book is not about me telling you the specifics of my happiness or the happiness of others because we are not the same. The indicator I use and the indicator that is a universal sign for all of us is the smile. Not a smile that we have forced, but one that springs onto our face in surprise. One that surges the emotion of happiness through our body, a smile that infects a room, inspiring the smiles of others.

In this book we will cover your "current state", or where you are today. Why are you the person you are now, and why does happiness at times seem so unreachable? From here, our journey will dive into the mental traps that hold us back from happier lives. Small daily mental shifts are next before wrapping it up with a bow in the form of those we choose to spend our time with.

The road to a happier life, of being the best possible version of yourself, is one that takes daily dedication. Most people would refer to me as a natural conversationalist. From the outside in, it would appear that having conversation throughout the day is easy and comes naturally for me. This could not be any further from the truth. Talk to my family and you will hear a story of shy Cal hiding behind his sister's leg, too scared to talk. Not being able to form sentences understandable by anyone outside of my family until I was six drove me into a very quiet and shy childhood. The last five years have been a conscious effort to build on these skills, and the realization has come from hard work that the quality of your relationships is directly tied to leading a happier life. The focus of Life Through the Eyes of a Smile is on creating a more open, deep-thinking mindset to create a life that is defined by the quantity and quality of smiles you leave behind over a lifetime. This is not a focus on plastering a smile on your face every single moment you are awake. That is completely unrealistic. This recipe requires having the bad days, ones void of any smile, to truly appreciate what does make us smile. Remembering the bad days and the events of those days are steps we have to take on this journey. We don't want to return to the same fast food store for 3 years straight, once a year because we conveniently forgot the pain of the meal or, went out on a limb and thought things might have gotten better. Another heavy focus will be on examining relationships for happiness and on interacting with others to find those with similar minds to celebrate this beautiful life with.

This book was not designed to dissect or target those who are naturals. Naturals are people who do not have to think about these concepts, they just happen. The few naturals I have spoken to really do not understand why I am writing on this topic. For them it is a no-brainer; a happier life comes because of the reasons in this book. Why write them down when they are so clear and programmed into the mind? Well, although the naturals will read this book and find humor from time to time, it is geared towards those who struggle with interaction, decisions and choices. Through many conversations with people who seem to be in a state of happiness and fulfillment, I have come across some who I would consider naturals. These are not the people I dissect and try to emulate, they have not come through trials and tribulations, it has just happened. The end state we are trying to get to is the same. However, this mindset was seemingly not developed over time in them. (Cue up your Lady Gaga voice): They were born this way. These people are rather boring to be around. The world turns into a cause-and-effect relationship with little experimentation. After all, why would they? It has always just worked out.

You will come away from this book with numerous small things to add to your day that will increase the quantity and quality of smiles over your lifetime. I encourage you to write them down, and when you are having a bad day, remember this book and try out one of the techniques within. Life Through the Eyes of a Smile is not just a book by some crazy person; it is a lifestyle, dedicated towards a successful life. A successful life must now take on a new meaning from the norms we have all grown up with, defining success as equal parts money and status. A successful life will now be weighed by the quality and quantity of smiles achieved and left behind over a lifetime.

You will find that portions of this book are written in the way I speak, which is by no means perfect. I see perfection as a trap, a trap that holds us back from the great things in life. If we wait for everything to be perfect before reaching out to the world, we will never fully let our brilliance shine. Just like smiles in our lives, if we try to always plan the perfect smile-inducing activities we will fail at ever achieving our brilliance. That being said, just as my voice shines through, so will my experience in rigorously testing all of the concepts within this book. The Calvin Simpson stamp of approval has been placed on every single concept that made it here, and trust me, I have failed at many, many things in the pursuit of life through the eyes of a smile. Nothing but the best of the best here. The road ahead is a long one, but so very worth it. Thanks for picking up this book and taking steps towards creating the most smile-filled version of yourself.

Effective Reading #LTESsecrets

If this is the first book you have picked up in a while, make sure you plan your next read now, which can be easily done by picking one of my suggested reads at the back! Stimulating thought and improving the way we think is at the core of asking the questions that will enable us to improve our lives.

Even if you put this book down half way through, make sure you pick up another. Reading will provoke inspiration and ground-breaking thought, and produce emotions that may have been hidden for a long time. At the moment, it feels like you will never forget the daring words littered across the page, and then two years later you try to remember one highlight of the book and...nothing. If you are an avid reader who has a strategy for remembering books, I suggest you skip right to the next section. If reading strategy sounds foreign to you, come along for this short ride; it is well worth your time.

The two most impactful books I have ever read were both from earlier on in my life. They were both complete mind-changers for the way I operated, and I have read them both multiple times since. If you asked me what my favorite parts of these books were, I could give you a great vague answer! The emotions tied to the books and overarching concepts will remain at a high level, but the memory of the details will fade. Think of a few details from three books ago that you read.

How are the finer details sticking to memory? I know these books are absolutely amazing and recommend them much of the time, but I do not have the slightest clue at the real big bang moments inside of them. This, to me, is an issue when recommending reads or when trying to really incorporate teachings into life. I know the book is great, but I cannot even pull a few teasers of content out of them.

This is where reading strategy comes into play. Books can be absolutely life-changing by the content that is within the pages. Being able to come back for motivation and inspiration is key to not forgetting lessons of the past. This is also a cool trail to look back on and see how you have grown over the years while in different stages of life and the alternate meanings you will find over these times. We all hated writing book reports in school; it only took me 20 years to realize the importance of writing them. A book report is one approach, keeping notes on each section/chapter as you go. Either do this throughout the pages or find the white space at the end of each chapter and fill in your details. Another option is a piece of paper with all your notes. This makes a fantastic bookmark and reference at the end of every read; just leave the custom book mark wedged in there. Once you turn the last page, take the time to then write a high level review of the book. Think of this like something you would be able to share with someone to give them a high level understanding. When you think something is cool, or inspiring, write it down!

How about in the e-reader world? If you read on an e-reader, make sure to use notes and highlighting whenever something catches your attention enough to slow you down, whether it is an A-ha moment, laugh, or pause for inflection. When in doubt, scribe it out! This is your chance to cut out the fluff and keep only the excitement. Think of writing this for your future self to look on and be re-motivated when solidifying the core concepts. Quotes are great; keep a section for top quotes, and when the year is over compile them together to see the quotes of the year. Looking to expand your social presence, or find it just plain fun to tweet or post photos of your reading endeavours? Post the most impactful words within your books to social media, including your notes, and use a custom hashtag to always be able to dig them up.

I use an approach of underlining impactful portions of every single book I read. I then write the page number of the underline on the front cover. This serves the purpose of not forgetting the most stimulating parts of your reading. It also provides a great quick refresher of the most meaningful portions of a book. This approach is to take the filler out and only hit the big bang moments with the overarching themes, keeping the book intact with just a quick reference of the front cover. Without a way to highlight A-ha moments it can be easy to lose the impactful details within books. Find what works for you, but just remember, you will not remember this line unless you make a conscious effort or action to.

Finding it tough to stay focused? Throw another distraction in the mix, music. Turn it on. In addition, there is not much that has not been dissected by Tim Ferris, if you are curious about increasing your reading speed while still retaining the same amount of knowledge. Google Tim Ferris's speed-reading. While you are at his site I also recommend taking a venture around; he has world-class content on achieving your personal best.

Lastly, remember that books, just like orange slices, are better when shared. Start a book-lending group with your friends and trade away. After you have both had a chance to read the content, share the impact it had on you, your favorite parts and any parts you feel are open for further discussion. You never know what will be uncovered when combining the views of two separate lenses!

Mindset

There was this thing called my mind. It talked me out of all these great things in life. Good thing I lost it.

Coming Up Through School and Into the Workforce Happiness U #LTESu

Bang bang, shots ring out across the yard. My sister and I duck as the bullets narrowly miss us, zinging over our heads. Charging with fear and a slight feeling of excitement, we head around the house, diving forward behind a tree to escape the attacker. This attacker is the infamous older brother, always in pursuit. Well, there was that one time I loaded the BB gun and chased him around the yard, but other than that there were never actual bullets in our guns, only imaginary ones. How much fun was it to play pretend as a child, whether it was cowboys and robbers or dress-up? An older brother and sister had me continually split between the two in a land of adventure.

Countless hours were dedicated to imagination, whether it was exploring the outdoors or playing with teddy bears. As children, our imaginations run rampant, and the bounds are limitless—limited only by those who are older around us, armed with the knowledge of what is best for us and expected of us. I can still remember the transition as a child away from using my imagination, when I learned that it was not the real world. When my older sister and I played with teddy bears, I noticed she always kept her imagination to play, but as a boy the expectation was higher to not play with teddy bears and to step into more of an adult male role. My brother Clay had experienced this as the oldest by five years. No doubt, the disappearance of imagination is a by-product of our education and the reliance on the correct answer on paper, with little room for creation or outside thinking. I tell this story not as a way to poke fun at Clay or education; losing our imagination and finding only one right answer to any question is cultural and embedded into our society.

I have addressed the loss of imagination from my experience and now I want you to stop and think. What were some of the most imaginative moments you had as a child? Think back to the younger years when time was spent thinking up games to play, characters to be, and no one to impress. When did your imagination begin to be tamed? Did you ever feel that your imagination was getting you into trouble, and was this a reason to start taming it? No longer do I try to tame my imagination and no longer do I look for one answer that would appease the masses. I now routinely search deep within my imagination for answers and look to open the doors to what I believe to be possible. Imagination will be your best friend in the journey to a happier life; together, you will have to question the norms of reality, journey down the path never travelled, and push the limits of those closest to you.

Now we reach our 20s. Graduation is nearing and soon, we will no longer have to live off of Ramen noodles. Soon it will be time for steak, that Audi, and the biggest house on the lake. A short 35 years lay ahead of us until it is time to claim the cake at the end of the tunnel! Instead, we get into the work-force and are stuck behind an Excel spreadsheet doing data entry. From the other angle we leave high school or college, hop into a career and are as technically sound as the people who have been there for 25 years in a short duration of 5 years. Talk about a dead-end for personal and career growth. When the CEO has not handed his chair over after five years we realize our expectations of career acceleration were totally unrealistic. Some careers will realize very fast growth up front, realizing every aspect of growth we could imagine. And then it hits a wall. There must be more and if there isn't, what do I do? Both of these problems are very tough to deal with and afflict most graduates after 5 years. The enticing cake at the end of the tunnel that seemed so easy to get to now seems to be more of an illusion than in reach.

The World Economic Forum performed a survey in the UK for a year between 2014 and 2015. The survey focused on general wellbeing: jobs, social activities, families and other overarching wellbeing questions. Guess when we are at the happiest in our lives? The peak physical years perhaps, when the world is at our feet? Perhaps in our 40s, when careers have been solidified and we conveniently are faced with a midlife crisis, stemming from too much money? Or would it be in our golden years, when we have the opportunity to reflect on life with dear friends and family?

On the other side, where would potential sources of dissatisfaction come from? Our 20s, when we are "putting in the time" buried behind a mountain of information to learn? Or in our 40s, when the children have moved out and thoughts of too few savings for retirement are mounting? Or in our 60s, when we have nothing to do all day except reminisce about the past?

And with no more need to fit any further words in this book we have our answer. The least happy time of our lives goes to … Drum roll … Ages 25-55, with the trough of our happiness occurring at age 35-45. And our happiness peak? The very summit occurs at age 65 with anything between 60 and 75 (end of the study) being the happies times of our lives. What does this mean to you? How do you interpret these results? I know when I first saw it, I was certainly going through a confusing time in my life, and although there were parts to be absolutely ecstatic at, I looked around me at the people in my life and it seemed pretty straightforward. Those who were in their working lives seemed pretty unhappy when compared to anyone under the age of 25 and those who were over 55.

I, being the data scientist I am, have come to some high level conclusions from simple visual interpretation of why we hit these lows and plummet into the unhappiest times during the working years of our life (25-55). We lose our sense of imagination in our 20s; everything becomes very concrete, and the expectations of becoming a professional and seasoned adult weigh heavy. There are no more games of cowboys and robbers, only hard work to find a thing called success. We get disoriented with the typical meaning of success being tied to

19

money and title. When we achieve these things it is odd; it is like the hole we were looking to fill has grown in size exponentially. Expectations along the lines of "Good things come to those who wait" run rampant. And the final conclusion is that our minds become overprotective, stifling us from progress and moving forward.

Work. It is work. If we could just skip it, then surely we would not be facing this rather large gap of disappointment. A world full of expectations in our careers and lives paints an endless cross-section of paths ahead with no clear direction on which one to take. Career advice such as "follow your passion" fills the mind during this time. Failures of the past are nearly hardcoded in; like touching a hot fire, we grow weary of second attempts. Our mindset and attitudes grow rigid. No ideas ever seem perfect enough to follow. Oftentimes, it feels as if we have nothing to contribute. We are doing nothing but learning from others.

Transitions #LTESrecipe

Life can be diced up and inspected over periods of time in many different ways. As life goes on, the chunks become bigger; as time increases, reflecting back brings us to times spent in towns, at jobs, and even lengths of times like when the kids were home. When we are younger and have been around for shorter periods of time, the years seem substantial and career moves massive. What I want to focus on now is the start of our decline into the Happiness U, where we really step off the deep end and do a tumble. We travel through school years at what seems to be the speed of molasses on a cold winter's day. We come out of our final education (high school or post-secondary) and enter the workforce. The key trigger to think of now is when you first settled into what, at the time, was seen to be a long-term job. We scramble to find our careers; the only real goal we have had since growing up has been to get into a good stable job and go. The focus all throughout school has been on what you want to be when you grow up, and when we get the job as the little red fire truck, the sense of satisfaction is massive. We begin our adult lives with the expectation checkmark checked we find a job. Next, we are most likely on track to get a nice car, buy a house, start a family and retire. All of these are phases of life most of us will move through. Routines start to form in our lives as we commute to and from work, wake up to the alarm clock (turns out work is not as easy as school to skip) and enjoy our weekends after hard fought days at work. Life becomes a recipe, taken from someone else's cookbook without asking any questions. Only 30 more years of this, and someone else's cake is at the end of our tunnel.

Rethinking Routine #LTESnew

A life full of routine drives to work, routine mornings, and routine weeks. Days become weeks, weeks become months, and months become years. How is this year starting for you?

Where did that year go? Where did the last 7 years go? The dreaded 7 year fear, having 7 years go past with little to no recollection. Do you ever wonder if you accidentally stepped into a time-travel device and sped through time with no real recollection? Perhaps the vehicle you step into every morning is actually a Delorean. To Barrett Jackson for a sale? What is the general story we hear over and over that has to do with the speed of time and our age? The older we get, the faster it goes. When you were a child, time seemed like it could not go any slower. When you are a child and growing up, much of the world is still new. Much of the world is still unknown.

Mindsets begin to close as we advance in life and for good reason. We find what works in life in all aspects, and through that process, we typically find what does not work. Work with two hours' sleep doesn't turn out that well, so we learn to avoid this at all costs. Waking up and then going right back to sleep also has its repercussions, so we do not incorporate that into a routine. Stage right enters the world's worst juice.

Think back to a time when you went out on a limb to try a new, eye-catching flavor of juice. Staring at you from the back of the fridge is old faithful. It looks a tad dull and dumpy today, so your eye wanders to a sleek new vibrant edition. Your mind starts to wander to the last time you made the poor choice to turn away old faithful for a shot in the near dark at a new option. One big gulp went down, a look of disgust crossed your face, a tear rolled down from your eye, and that juice that once looked at you so enticingly now resembles your own worst enemy. The thought then jumped to mind: "I am never veering away from the usual again. The usual satisfies me. I would have never had this awful experience had I stayed in my comfort zone."

Old Faithful

If you have ever searched for something out of the ordinary, rather than Old Faithful, you certainly have had a few adventurous thoughts. "How much better could things be? What could I be missing out on?" Perhaps you witnessed someone else enjoying their beverage and you thought to yourself, "Wow, I want what she is having." These thoughts boil down to the desire to try something new and out of the ordinary, so why don't you? Mental hurdles are constructed along the lines of, "Remember last time I tried something new? Big mistake." Or, "No it couldn't possibly be any better and besides, I am perfectly happy with the experience I have now, why change?"

Electrify Your Routine

The options we face everyday are numerous and constantly in a state of change. It really is no wonder we stick to one choice after all the botched trials. The sting of the betraying juice is all too fresh in our mouths and we settle back into our comfort zone with Old Faithful. After the weeks go by, a small wandering thought creeps back into our minds. How good could that newly arrived eye catching juice possibly be? When the decision between old faithful and the unknown inevitably arises again, go with the unknown. If you stumble upon a bottle of face twisting juice, smirk at the experience you just had and dream of the next big opportunity that lies ahead (after you forget the taste bud pain).

Go out and try something new tomorrow, no matter how trivial the change may seem. It might not work out, but on the other hand, it could be the best experience you have had in a long time. The choice lies with you. Use your calendar for a reminder if you have to. Type in "Try something new" and have it ring three times during your day.

"Our time here is limited, what we chose to do with that time however, is not." - Jeb Corliss

Chances are, you haven't tried any green juice lately but the chances are very good you have thought about modifying your routine recently in the hopes of inspiring an intriguing new change. As life goes on, it becomes routine to stop searching for open doors and instead start thinking of reasons why we should be closing those doors that are open. Early on in the circus life of an Elephant they are chained to poles. They try to bust loose from their anchors but are simply not strong enough to. In time, after many failed attempts to bust loose, they learn to stop trying. They belief that they will never be able to break their chains is set into their minds from a young age and that belief is no longer challenged. Even as they grow much taller and much stronger. Over time the chains would be no match for the strength of an elephant but the belief instilled at the young age holds them back from ever trying again. Many cases have been documented where fully developed elephants have lost their lives in fires because they do not believe they can break free from the chains that would stop them as a young elephant, but are no match for themselves when fully grown. Humans are not much different than elephants in the fact that we also develop our beliefs from lessons we have learned in the past. There is one piece we routinely forget in this picture however, and that piece is our personal growth. We are not the same people as we were in the past, we grow.

The world around us no longer seems new as we repeat the same tasks over and over at work, commute the same routes, and settle into our comfort zones. Time-travel is one of our best indicators of a life that is on complete speed mode and that smiles are most likely slipping by us. We will look at slowing down time when we get to the mentality section, shortly after the chapter where we plan our funerals!

Flex 40 #LTESratherBe

Diving into one of the largest sources of routine in our lives, we find the 40-hour workweek. We are taught to get to work, do the same old thing, have the same old water cooler conversation and hope we ride in the elevator with someone worth staring at or latch onto the excitement that stems from the lives of others, often taking the form of Dr. Phil episodes! Think about the typical day in your life at work. What was the highlight of this week? What was the highlight of the day? Are your days only interesting when something happens to you? Or when others provide the entertainment? When was the last time you were the source of entertainment and joy? Alright, enough thinking about yourself and the boring days at work, let's move over to someone who surely has more fun than all of us put together: wild man, billionaire extraordinaire Richard Branson.

Branson is always making the headlines for some sort of mischief in all of his photos with his signature smile from ear to ear. What is one of the most well-known ingredients in his recipe to success? Having fun and promoting flexible work environments. Whether he leads by example from an island, atop a mountain, or cutting through the seas, he has worked and lived his life from all over. He brings together "life at work" and "life outside of work" into just plain and simple life. His approach is on a grandiose scale, riding on ships, balloons and in the air with all types of antics. From us these look like major changes, all of which are too massive to ever hope to accomplish. The part we are missing, however, is that for Richard these are just small changes in his day, and at one point in his life, they were all completely out of reach. Just like these are small changes and updates in his day today, we all have this same power on our own scale. The only difference here is he is having his fun on a grandiose scale.

We have the ability to have this same magnitude of fun but, as it relates to our scale, not Sir Richard's. This is one of the great quandaries we will cover; most things look out of reach to us because they are really far out of reach as to where we are now. We tend to forget that we all start the same, and the unfortunate/ fortunate truth is we can all create what we desire over time. We just have to place the conscious effort into it. Take this thought to your job this week, and play a friendly game of "Where would you rather be right now?" Or, "If you could step into Richard Branson's shoes for the day what would you do?"

I Wonder What Is on Netflix? #LTESsmileCarbs

A h, the day is over, now time to head home and do...what? The time has arisen to think harder into the to-do list, perhaps even to pull something from the elusive, I-should-really-try-this list. Coming home from a hard day's work, the couch passes along a look, almost like that of a child or favorite pet gives you when you return home: "I have been waiting for you all day!" It has readily prepared itself with perfect butt grooves, inviting you to sit on down and just soak it all in. One more episode it is! The New Year then rolls around and the long list from last year has not been touched since March. We know it is easier, and generally feels nicer, to sit on the couch, but does finishing another series on Netflix have the same emotional connection as stepping towards a better version of ourselves? Let's say we have been putting off signing up for that online course for a few months, going to that fun-looking fitness class, or meeting up with that long lost friend. Which will have higher emotional value when completed? Initially, the temptation and ease of staying seated in front of that TV and watching Netflix will rule; however, when it ends, how will we feel? I think we can all align with the Netflix effect. It seemed like such a good idea up front out of pure short-term pleasure.

You may be thinking: well Calvin, Netflix provides some of the most routine smiles in my life. Not all smiles are made the same and the easiest way to think of this is in the form of carbs: good carbs and bad carbs. They both provide us with the resultant energy we are looking for; however, some come with a lot more waste by-product, proving to be more troublesome for us. The bad carbs here of course being personal development. Just kidding, you are better than that. The bad carbs here are Netflix; they provide us with the smile and relaxation we are looking for in the short term, but they provide very little return for us in the long term. Flipping over to personal development, we see little returns immediately. The good carbs of smiles provide low returns in the short term but provide mega returns in the long run. Picture binge watching Netflix for 5 years straight, you are happy in the short term but how does it feel in the long run? Think of a good carb such as working out, in the short term it can suck but, in the long run the feeling is oh so fulfilling. Dedicate 30 minutes a day, starting today to reading, physical activity or time with a loved one. Insert one of those great sayings about: If I had only started 365 days ago... (Math tells me that is over a full week of time, over a year, dedicated to yourself for only 30 minutes a day. SMOKING DEAL!)

I Just Don't Know What to Do
#LTESstork

Perhaps one of the biggest blocks we have ever faced to pushing forward in life is the "I do not know what to do" mindset. Others seem to have found a passion, yet the stork has just not dropped mine off at the door. This is the feeling of not being challenged, of not contributing or being valuable enough to contribute. Termed by Viktor Frankl as the existential vacuum, this term stands for looking at life and not finding any meaning or purpose. This is the "I am not good enough" phase that can be programmed into us from a few failures, which eventually becomes internal destructive dialogue. Have you ever been kicking around on a weekend and thought, "I have absolutely nothing to do"? Or have you ever wished you had a sport to practice, a job you enjoyed, or people in your life who loved you? Another nice, fancy term that comes to mind is Sunday Neurosis. Sitting on the couch thinking what am I doing, what is this all for? On the most typical leisure day we find ourselves often winding down from the weekend, readying for the week and thinking to ourselves, "Well that weekend was alright, but this week ahead is going to suck."

Any man or woman who has a "why" to live for can make it through almost any how. Take Viktor Frankl, for example. His "why" to live through the Holocaust was to share his learnings, and in going through this period, he was also able to field test and observe his hypothesis in action. He found that those who focused on the how, quickly lost the drive to push forward with no real value left in the day. Now relating this back into our day, how much easier does work become when we have an event at the end of the day? Perhaps even a holiday coming up, or a sporting event or just generally anything to look forward to that is a passion or interest outside of work? Now on the other hand, how about those days where you actually looked forward to going to work? Maybe there was something like a job promotion, celebration of a co-worker or another celebration. Figuring out a "why" to all aspects of life will be the biggest aid you can find in leading a happier and more fulfilled life.

"He who has a why to live can bear almost any how"

-Friedrich Nietzsche

Okay, so I see there is still nothing for me to do on Sundays. How do I find this passion thing? And can I just speed this process up and pay to have one dropped off at my door? It seems like it would be easier this way. We are bombarded with people telling us to follow our passion out there, and this advice typically comes when we are frustrated that our job is not providing enough opportunity or our work's not being appreciated. Right out of the gate from our last school, we are told to find our passion in our career and just follow it. So we get into an organization and slog through work that seems meaningless, all the while trying to find passion. Passion driven from a pat on the back, title changes, and money raises.

Oddly, this passion thing is pretty confusing, and over time we become pretty sure it is tied to none of these aspects. The desire for more comes as life drags by and no real sense of accomplishment arrives.

Day after day, as we perform the routine tasks, our career trajectory seems much like standing in line and grabbing your number with all your co-workers. A few great ideas rise to your mind but your own fear of success and fear of standing out from the rest hold you back. A tipping point arises when the life of a yogi or passion becomes the magnet too strong to ignore. A passion burns deep from within and a world of quotes bombard you, all reaffirming you are on the right path to follow your true passion to have success in life. How many people do you know who have followed their passions to live the life they most desire? Now how many of these people made it from scratch? I do not mean from scratch as waking up one day in junior high school with a burning passion to repair computers or write books. I mean they left what they fell into to pursue their true passion without working at it prior to building up the necessary skills, connections, and credibility. I am sure not very many; it simply does not work this way.

As Cal Newport puts it so elegantly in So Good They Can't Ignore You, it is necessary to first build career equity in your desired field. This means attaining select skills that very few have and honing them to up your personal value, or career equity. The skills you hone have to be of interest you, which means you are willing to put in extra time with them learning and improving consciously. Over time, as you hone these skills, you will naturally start to pair them with other skills you have attained in life. These combined skills as a whole will take on your signature. No one has the same background as you; therefore, your influence and your approach will be completely unique. Building on these desirable unique skills is where we find our passions in life, not by simply waiting around for the passion person to drop one off one day. Pairing these skills in unique ways to you, operating in border realms and pushing the limits of these borders is where massive success is found.

Now, what if you absolutely hate your job and already have skills in another area that you have been jonesing to follow? Abandon ship and full sails ahead? No, because no other ship exists beside you to carry you forward. This is where career equity comes into play and my advocacy for experimentation within your career path. The question begs to be asked, what are the chances you graduate and land in the job that is perfect for you and will provide the most smiles in your life? Pretty slim, and it does not take a well-known statistician named Calvin to teach you this.

It is actually very simple. The world out there is big and we, alongside our circle of influence, are very small. The approach that has been well documented for a successful career change requires a two-pronged approach or, the dreaded multi-tasking! Two careers at once. With our new found bad carbs for happiness we have the opportunity to introduce happy happy smile carbs in the form of our new found passion. In time, the frustration from holding down two careers will build. However, your career equity will begin to build in your new path. With this building career equity we are looking to surpass our skills, reputation, and monetary intake. When this happens, or is very close to happening, it is time to dive in with both feet. No different than proving a market before developing a product, we have to prove that what we are looking at transitioning over to is sustainable. Holidays, freedom of the workplace, and dedication to loved tasks all become easier and much more achievable as personal value increases.

Okay, so you may still have no clue where to start this search for the all-elusive passion. Throw on your crocodile hunter hat, khaki shorts, and Aussie accent, it is passion-hunting time! In the pages ahead lies our recipe: trying new things outside of your pre-existing comfort zone paired with providing value outward in the form of creation. [closes book, life solved]

Creation vs Expectation Mindset
#LTEScreation

We have now begun to think about all those people out there who tell us to follow our passion. Take Steve Jobs, for example. If he had followed his passion out of college, he would have been a seasoned yogi. Instead, he took his unique sales skills, paired them with similar minds behind hardware, and voila! A few years later, we had an amazing company in the form of Apple computers. No stork drop-off, and no one sneaking into his career garden planting the seed of passion.

Since you will most likely be dozing off into the book here (I know I am) after the first sprint of reading, and since it is very likely that work shows up tomorrow, I want you to close this book and type the following into YouTube "Jim Carrey MUM" and watch it, even if you have already seen it. It is all too easy to expect everything in the world and then become overwhelmed when our wildest desires do not come true at precisely the right time. As Tony Robbins put it, "Trade expectation for appreciation." I would like to change it to and have you think of "Trade expectation for creation." You have something special in you. Identify what it is, and when you find it, offer it to the world. We have all pondered the following in our career: "Where am I going? What are the plans for me? When will I be promoted?" These are all very expectation and extrinsic-based motivations. What can the company offer me? I demand to know, I am a valuable worker! Or we might think, "The world has nothing to offer me. Everyone else gets these awesome things placed at their feet and not me. Not the slightest thing." When you find these questions popping into mind you must ask yourself the following:

What are you offering the world? While we are at work we focus on what we can create, leaving behind the expectation for what the day will give us. Instead, ask what value you can provide in this day. Celebrate successes this way instead of feeling ripped off because the day provided nothing. This is the "aha" moment when you hear many workers say, I just stopped caring and everything got better. When the word "caring" is used here, it is used in the context of "I stopped caring about what others thought, and I just focused on what I could create."

Alongside the creation mindset comes a very important feedback mechanism, our performance and personal growth. Not the score on the clock.

External Validation #LTESscore

How do you know if you are going down the right path in life and business? How do you measure it? Expecting feedback from individuals for stellar performance? Perhaps some sort of external feedback, like the score on the board in sports? When judging growth and performance using only external measures, more fog rather than clarity is easily introduced.

Keep the keys in your hands and eyes off of the score

Life is all about people and working together. However, beware when the word "they" starts being used excessively in your vocabulary: "They are so lucky, they seem to get everything, I wonder what they did to get that." This word is a signal of relying solely on others to give feedback on your actions. You are driving your own vehicle, and when you only rely on others to provide direction, you are handing the keys and ability to steer over to another. These are some common things we hear when "they" starts to take over your thinking:

They wasted my time...

Whether it be unclear expectations or missed meetings, this can be one of the most frustrating to handle. Have a backup plan for your time in case the person is a no-show or late. I personally always have a book on me. Be clear on the purpose and desired outcome of the meeting, which will minimize confusion in sitting down and making the most out of both parties' time. Like in price negotiation, things work a lot smoother when you both understand an acceptable dollar value.

They did not accept...

Is that person from another planet!? Perhaps it was a business networking event, a new introduction, or tip-top proposal. Everything was making so much sense until it fell absolutely dead. In life, we can do all the right things and never be accepted by all, nor should we want to. If you listened to the other person, understood their position and put all the right work in, then that is a communication success! Sales-folk, you live this one day in and day out. Do you have any other advice?

How about new relationships? You may ask, "Why aren't they calling, I wonder what I did?" This is a trap we get caught up in assuming that others should be thinking about us as much as we think about ourselves. The questions wrap up into this all-consuming wonder of what is going on in the other persons head and what did we do wrong. This is the point at which we have handed our keys over to another to set direction in our lives, instead of us setting the direction.

They do not value my work...

Typical in the workforce are the underappreciated worker and their abilities. People often think, "I do not receive enough thank-yous for my work and it is almost like no one knows the effort I put into this organization!" Did you put your best effort into it, did you learn and grow in the process? Your results always pay off in the long run, and when you are performing at your best, results will always shine through, regardless of others seemingly taking notice or not. Next up to bat is that person in life who no one has any idea of what is going through their head, the difficult one. Whether it be at work, a friend or even an acquaintance, it is all too easy to get wrapped up in thought around how to deal with this person. Again, see ya later keys!

The opinions of other people are a feedback mechanism to our own improvement, that lies within the realm of external validation. John Wooden solidified the following concept into his record-setting basketball teams—you can play the best game of your life and still lose on the board. This does not mean that you need to change everything you are doing, and it certainly does not give you the "opportunity" to feel bad about yourself. Instead, looking internally for validation, ask yourself if you put forth your best effort. If so, you can be nothing short of proud at the new personal best that has been achieved, forgetting the misleading score on the board.

Like any topic, there are two ends of a stick, and extremes are rarely the best choice. You are on the right path in business and life when you weigh your performance most heavily through personal growth and dedication placed into the task. Keep your keys in hand, and focus internally --> externally, not the other way around.

Identity #LTESbestSelf

Who will I be when I walk out the door today?

Alongside life transitions come different versions of ourselves. As life goes on, we change with our age, environment, and network. We even change from a Monday morning to a Friday afternoon to being hungry and sleep-deprived. Alongside these changes comes the high likelihood we will struggle with decisions we used to make easily, confused between many versions of ourselves and which answer is best suited to the moment.

Let's take a look at one of the most major transitions we have to navigate in life, exiting our last years of school to enter the workforce. We develop our view of the world at this point, mostly out of what others tell us we should be expecting. Much of the world is new, so this is how we learn, from others. Where the confusion arises is the branch from the theoretical world, how we expect the world to be, as forecasted by another. Fortunately, we do not all experience the world the same, and we are quickly thrown into positions where having our own opinion is needed. This current opinion is formed from our past experiences. Looking into the life transition we make after graduating college, we find the career influence taking effect.

We all know this to be a confusing time. For me, it was best shown through a group of new employees taking an Insights quiz. This quiz consists of a multitude of questions with multiple choice answers. The answers you provide bring insight into who you are, describing traits and characteristics outputting a diagnosis of personality. The answers and diagnosis of who I was were quite shocking, they had nailed me. For others the diagnosis was way off. What stuck with me was the response one person had to the mis-diagnosis, they mentioned they did not know who they were supposed to be when answering the questions. The person they are at work or, the person they are at home. I remembered going through the exact same confusion starting my career, I was two people during my day; one person at work and one person at home. I took this test after going through the immediate life transition that occurs entering the work force. I had already been through the awkward time of being one person at work and another person outside of work, I was simply just Calvin. This change was largely driven from a shift in environment, that was a move between cities; it required a move to reinvent myself to be truer to myself. Not working hard days at a job with very low drive and lacking motivation. This ate at me, and I retaliated as most do with hard swings back and forth of extreme work and extreme relaxation. This was needed however, the transitions also needed to slow. That landed me in Calgary as much more centered and true to myself. Without actually spanning the limits of who we are, a single identity, who we really are is not easy to find.

Look at Joe De Sena, the founder of the Spartan race. His passion to push boundaries inspired him from a pool and concrete construction career to Wall Street to an early retirement to taking part in boundary testing marathons. Seemingly his identity changes as he moves through careers, this is not the case. He identifies with testing people mentally and physically, seeing how far other's will push their limits. In turn, the testing he puts people through gives them a heavy dose of self-worth. Whether they finish the race at the front of the pack or in the back, they are proving to themselves their self worth in pushing their own boundaries. In the story that all too often plays, boundaries are set by others unrealistically early in life in an effort to grab onto a path of someone else, leaving a struggle for identity in discovering realism and normalcy. Often the identity that is easiest to grab onto is one of expectation. We are taught that you must identify with your career. In the Insights course, it became clear that not all assessments were bang on. At the end, I felt I had been read like a book, and for others it was a complete miss. The comment came out that it was not clear who they were supposed to be when answering the questions. Was I supposed to be the person I am at work, or the person I am outside of work? This creates a serious internal struggle, delaying and thwarting the ability to make any decisions.

There is a skill to acting, however, the dangers become very real when identifying oneself. Consistency in messaging, covered further in the community section, is one of the strongest traits that draws us to a person. Consistency in messaging includes the ability to stand up for ones beliefs and to work towards them. If we are constantly operating out of multiple beliefs or values, it creates confusion not only internally but on the outside as well. It becomes difficult for others to like us, and thus difficult to attract consistent positive emotion to our lives. We are at our best when operating from a core set of values and beliefs. When we operate against our beliefs and values, a rift is thrown up within our bodies, confusing emotions. Having difficulties and internal struggles? Use one simple question to yourself to set direction. What would the best version of myself do? This question will bring you back in line to one identity when you are torn between two actions and two versions of yourself.

Things Are in Reach #LTESfishStories

What seems just out of reach in life has been out of reach at one point in time, which leads us to believe it will always be out of reach. Life is a continuous learning process in which failure to reach what seems just at our fingertips is so real. We train ourselves to not get hurt again, for lack of better words. We then place that far out goal into the depths of our mind, and if it is there for too long, it keeps working further and further away, lengthening the gap that has to be closed. It's just like our elephants in chains. An active imagination is needed when this happens; we "know" things in life can be just out of reach, and this will limit our belief that we can get whatever it may be. If we can visualize it as possible, our subconscious will commit and do everything possible to take us there. We must learn to grow our arms and grasp what seemed out of reach in the past. In Jim Carrey's 2014 speech at the Maharishi University of Management (MUM)commemoration, he urges all in attendance to ask the universe for what they desire.

Ask the universe, and work towards it. Open the door in your head, and when the door opens, just walk through it. Don't worry if you miss your cue—doors continually open. Why ask the universe? Because we will rarely have the immediate answer for how to get what we want. Through addressing our desires, good things will happen. Jim Carrey's example was asking the universe for a hot rod red racer bike with a stylish banana seat. Two weeks later, he came home to a brand new ride on his balcony. Hope can be a dangerous drug; however, faith is a cure to your limiting beliefs. Not faith in a religious context—I mean faith in yourself to become better and better, surpassing any limiting beliefs fear imposed on you. When faith is alive and well within us, we forget about creating the perfect plans for our future, and we start grabbing hold of the end vision, worrying less about how things should happen.

Usually, when we see doors open in life we start to close them instead of daring to walk through them, as it is not our vision of the perfect path forward we see. How tricky our mind is that we talk ourselves out of walking through these doors into opportunity. Alan Watts inspired me when talking of a golden age in religion. He paints the picture of time and as more of it passes, the more the concept of a golden age passes us by. Things become seemingly farther and farther out of reach— how can we ever create what has happened in the past? They were so much smarter, stronger, hard working and [insert generic one-upper word here] than we are now. The over exaggerated fish stories of the past become so great we lose all faith in creating anything that will come near to the accomplishments of the past. We look into the past and are discouraged, often times into not even trying, because we do not see the ability to create anything that will be of comparison. The question has to be asked: who psycho-analyzed Freud? So much in life is right for others but just out of reach for us.

Let's take a look at Eckhart Tolle, for example. He is well known for being one of the most patient and understanding

48

people in the world. Heck, you could probably run him over on purpose with your car to find him trying to help you get the car off of him because it was just what needed to happen. When we have idols like this, no wonder everything seems out of reach. We only see a chasm that has to be crossed, not the very long path up the side of a mountain to a bridge that crosses the same chasm. We all have the ability to create something much bigger than the past.

Vision #LTESimagine

Got vision? Yes, I have it; it consists of my two eyeballs and the world they project. This is one of those words that helps keep life out of reach for us and is also rather confusing. Vision is something that comes up from time to time, and if we admit not to having one we then become the weird person in the room. Ooh, Calvin doesn't have a defined vision, trouble everyone!

First of all, let's take the mask off of this word and define it for what it is. A vision is simply the ability to re-ignite a long lost ability from our childhood—using our imaginations. We have to imagine a better place we will be in the future, a better version of who we are now. The stronger our imagination, the stronger our emotional tie will be driving us forward. Anticlimactic? Maybe. But it's so often tossed around that you need a vision statement to live by, so what is yours? Those who have it stand proudly behind it, grasping hold of this thing that will solve all future problems. Companies all have great generic vision statements of making the world a better place through stock reason A, B and C. Having a vision is of utmost importance in our pursuit of life through the eyes of a smile. This vision needs to show us being the very best we can be in any given situation—a vision so ripe with imagination, so vivid that emotion is inspired and action is created. Once you see the potential you have and what you can create, it is nearly impossible to ignore it. The vision within life through the eyes of a smile is to create a world in which the quality and quantity of our smiles in amplified. How do we get there? That is all up to each one of us. It all starts with an imagination and the stronger the imagination, the stronger the emotional tie, and the greater likelihood we will create our vision.

Thwarting Your Mind #LTESpicnics

Avision is nothing without action except for a cool dream. The best intentions in the world go nowhere running on the gas of good intentions. We need to dig deeper to help our future selves by making action easier and less emotionally painful. Progress: we want it, but we are unsure how to get there after so many failed attempts. We try and try, using the same methods to get what we want within the same environment. As our friend Albert Einstein laid it out for us the definition of insanity is "doing the same thing over and over again and expecting different results". If we continually see the same falter points, use the same methods, and function within the same environments, then why is it not easy to learn and progress? Because all of these conditions can be easily camouflaged and difficult to discover. Turns out just by reading the definition of insanity it is not actually that easy to become sane and progress in life. By examining our past behaviors and habits, we can set ourselves up for success on the paths that lie ahead of us. Use this approach when you are having troubles getting things done. Map out your mood and environment, look for traps, and set up picnics.

Let's take a look at a few snapshots of myself in time, alongside snares or traps I commonly trip myself up with (self-laid traps), and picnic baskets (personal aids) I can set to assist myself on the journey ahead.

I Am Not a Morning Person

Upon waking, the questions of what day it is, where I have to be, and what I have to do dominate my headspace. Stumbling out of bed, I trudge through the morning routine of hygiene, dressing, and getting to the task at hand—let's say it's getting to work today. Confusion, no problem solving skills, and "where on earth is the matching sock?" describe my mood well during this snapshot.

Snares - No lunch or breakfast prepared. Low energy. No schedule in sight.

Picnic baskets - A prepared lunch the night before. A review of the day ahead laying out tasks to complete. Placing the coffee pot on a timer. Getting a good night's sleep. Perhaps an alarm clock that picks me up and places me in the shower.

By thwarting my mind during this snapshot in time, I see the benefits of added energy and a much calmer mind.

Chronically 5 Minutes Late

How fast can I make it to work today? I can easily make it in 10 minutes, eclipsing my average time of 15. Today is the day each leg grows two feet, and I will certainly hit all the crosswalks just right. James Bond-like, I manoeuver under the radar to my desk. "Can this elevator move any slower?" and delusions of the ability to manipulate time describe my mindset well during this snapshot.

Snares - Thinking today is the day I bend time. Justification that if everyone else is late, then I can be too.

Picnic Baskets - Setting my alarm 10 minutes early. Ask a co-worker who is chronically early to hold you accountable. It is all too easy to justify to yourself why you are late, so try the co-worker friend who is not so easily persuaded.

"If you can be 5 minutes late you can be 5 minutes early." - Eugene Simpson. By thwarting my mind during this snapshot in time I see the immediate benefit of less stress in my life.

Dishes in the sink

Dish Mountain lies in front of me. Yes, I forgot to examine the apartment for a dishwasher prior to purchase. Simply thinking about the task that lies ahead induces emotional pain. With Dawn at my side, I fight the war, sustaining damage the whole way throughout. Thoughts of "I hate this task," "when will this be over?" and "I cannot wait to leave this task alone for another week" dominate my mind.

Snares – "I will get to it later" mindset. Letting the pile grow, and grow, and grow.

Picnic Baskets - Eating only after all the dishes in the sink have been cleaned (it is arguably impossible to eat before the dishes are done). Fill the time in between cooking with cleaning dishes to limit the pain of cleaning to short, manageable durations.

By thwarting my mind during this snapshot in time, I see the immediate effects of an uncluttered environment, providing ease of mind.

Have a nagging problem or desire for change? Try thwarting your own mind by empathizing with yourself during past situations. Learn your behaviors and how to best work with them. Identify snares, or actions that add difficulty to making progress, and don't water a slope you are trying to climb. Identify ways to ease your journey through problematic situations. Leave your future self picnic baskets to maintain resilience and recharge your batteries in troublesome situations. Progress is yours to take hold of.

Our Perfect Self #LTESbuffet

Now that we have our minds thinking about the action we can take, it comes time for planning and the dreaded perfect self. We have to come to grips with the fact we will never be the perfect self we picture in the mirror—never having to falter, being the suave, charismatic, brilliant, citizen of the decade, and making every decision to serve this version. We will not weigh up to our perfect self, and when this becomes the expectation we close down to the world, which stops us from ever stepping out and presenting ourselves in our full light. Perhaps it is in a group of friends or co-workers, a question or comment lights a fire in us and then the self-doubt creeps in and we start asking, "What if? What if I have some of the details wrong? What if I stumble when talking and freeze up?" We then conclude this with the thought that we would rather just keep our opinion to ourselves and not risk tarnishing the perfect image that is our self in front of the group. Perhaps it is a day you were really looking to getting a workout in and you just aren't feeling 100 percent, a sure sign of not getting the perfect workout. Our perfect self will look at these situations, raise its nose, lift the pinky off of the martini glass and shun any half attempt for being below ourselves, not worthy of them. Our best self, on the other hand, will look at the situation and its details for a level of understanding.

Before we go on our adventurous phone call we have to paint the picture of what our best self looks like and what our perfect self looks like. Our perfect self lives at the farthest edge of reason. Our perfect self thinks, "No worries, happiness is all over and the world as we see it, is everyone else see's it. Life is perfect." Let's say we are baking a cake that is our best possible self. We know the recipe is all thrown off from the perspective of our perfect self but what do we add to dilute this recipe back into the realm of ideal? The key ingredient we need: realism.

Serving your best and perfect self at a buffet

Starting off at the buffet line, our perfect self leads the way. Heaping servings of every portion and a singular focus on only that item is the lead trait. Coming through the end of the buffet line the plate is completely overflowing, no worries, our perfect self can easily stomach all these tasks. Next up to bat is our best self, staring down the road ahead it is clear there is a lot of food. Past experience tells us that our eyes and wants are bigger than we can handle at one time. The routine favorites are chosen in manageable portions, and those dishes you have always wanted to try but have never gotten around to grace the plate now. You observe this behaviour from afar. What are the chances that these two look-alikes sit in your section? Yet they are headed that way, and off to the table it is. Sitting down, your perfect self's plate looks even more perfect up close—all your favorite food from the station, and in those extravagant quantities you have always desired … Mmm, I wonder what he will get for dessert. Looking over to the plate of your best self, the quantities of your favorites seem a little small. There are a few things on the plate that you have been looking at trying for a while but just have never gotten around to. Interesting, but it seems a little too far out there and a little too slim with the choices.

Drinks are in order, what can I get you two? Perfect self starts firing again with all the favorites (What are your 3 favorite drinks? Imagine them and their ultimate perfection) and your best self, (insert a favorite drink here, one fit for a routine dinner). As the drinks come, you start to overhear conversation. Your best self is chatting about the week ahead and how it has been much easier to find balance after putting some thought into what matters most. You overhear one of the areas of life has been put off for the time being, but you know it will return. Ooh, that is a serious blow, must suck to have to leave something behind, even if it is only temporary. Moving over now to your perfect self, everything you have ever wanted graces this list and wow you have it all right now, it seems almost too good to be true.

Our perfect self will look at the world and every situation as manageable and deserving of being in our life. There is no such thing as burnout or imbalance in these shoes. The world is ours, and we can have it all right now. The perfect self has the life of our wildest dreams, which seems a thousand years away, so why put all the effort in to get there? Chances are we will never ever get there anyway. Further thinking in life and life through the eyes of an upside-down smile are all too close here. Bridging over to our best self, we find a world shaped out of realism. Every situation is not manageable on our own and under short durations. Not everything in our life will receive our 100 percent; this is not realistic. Burnout is a real thing and if we try to give our 100 percent across the board we will experience hitting a wall. This wall cannot be passed without rest and sacrifice in certain areas of life.

When comparing the perspectives of our two selves, it is rare we will ever choose the silver edition when the gold edition stares us down because, let's face it, why would we ever settle for second in the game of ourselves? Whenever we sit around and dream up better versions of ourselves, or what we should be doing that day or month, it is easy to get as far away from where you are right now as possible. Why not? It feels great. We are smart, and we typically invest in longer periods of time, such as yearly goals. The problem here is that we overinflate our desire in the task with the desire we are feeling now. Twelve books a month? That is a massive investment in time, and you better enjoy reading and know to cut losses with bad books. This is the perspective of our perfect self, the yogi, mental giant superstar that can activate right now and for the rest of the year on command. Adding that much needed dash of realism to our recipe: we can get there, but it is not tomorrow. When we set wild expectations from the perspective of our perfect self we are bound to always fall short, leading to disappointment and demotivation. We develop the belief that we cannot achieve anything more in our life after continued failure. We learn to not go around hot fires after being burned. Why would we try for a goal after falling flat on our face? We certainly are not all entrepreneurs and not all like those determined quotes. What we do all have in us, however, is a desire. It may just be a flickering candle light sometimes, but it will not go out. How do we add fuel to that fire? By proving to ourselves that we can actually do it, we can get closer to the seemingly out-of-reach goal. Break it down into smaller chunks and start knocking them off. Start proving your self-worth with mini celebrations.

Take Steps Not Leaps #LTESsteps

Have you ever been enamored by a potentially life-changing goal, just to watch it fall flat on its face two weeks later? Your intention is there, you have your best interests in mind, so why did you not succeed?

Taking over the world

When we are in a passionate state of mind, we feel we could create change big enough and fast enough to take over the world. Our old habits are tossed to the side, and decisions are made on the spot. We are inspired to make a difference in that very moment. Do we have what it takes to carry this passion forward? Most times we simply do not. By the time this thought festers for a week or two, we have all but forgotten our initial passion, and we slip back into our old routine.

Leaps

Mental leaps, just like physical leaps, will lead to overtiring and a higher likelihood of giving up. In the heat of the moment we may think we can take on the world with one fell swoop. Instead, our batteries deplete to empty, and we abandon the task at hand. To take a personal example, I have been saying I will learn Spanish for over a year now. How close am I to my end goal? About as far as a person could possibly be. Multiple times I have sat down and spent four hours Googling "Spanish series with English subtitles". Seemingly finding the right fit, two hours of top quality Spanish daytime TV passes by. A rush of content satisfies my emotion, I mentally pat myself on the back, and move on. Three weeks later, I remember that I have not taken a single step since the last Español Gossip Girl binge.

Dan Ariely is a professor at Duke University specializing in behavioural economics, and he is best known for attacking the topic of irrationality. Dan has dedicated his life to the understanding of people's actions after an incident he experienced as a child. He was involved in an Israeli youth group growing up, and at one of the demonstrations, there was an accident. This explosion involved magnesium flares, and he sustained burns on over 70% of his body. He spent the next almost 3 years in the hospital with little to no skin. Daily bandages had to be removed from his body, leading to excruciating pain. The process was high intensity spread over a short duration, the typical "rip the Band-Aid off" experience. Dan knew a slower process was much easier on him; however, the hospital staff thought this was wrong. There was no winning for him. Dan had a question still stuck in his mind when exiting the hospital: "Can you manage an experience for a patient differently so that it creates less pain?" Dan started researching this question in the lab by delivering pain to people in different ways. Dan would administer pain from high to low, low to high and administer pain over differing durations with differing intensities. Dan used a scale of 0-100 to then rate the subjective pain of each test subject. The scores ranked consistently with his theory from his experience; longer duration with lesser pain was better than short duration and high pain.

Where does this fit into our lives when looking at creating change, primarily around habits? When we are planning our future goals and visions we find an anchor point, such as removing a band-aid, and then place a duration on it. In being true to ourselves, we like to typically shorten this deadline to prove we can do it, hasten the process to get to the excitement quicker. This Band-Aid approach of high intensity and low duration is setting ourselves up for failure. By lengthening the time we invest in getting to our goals, we keep the intensity much more bearable.

Giant Snowballs

What is the best way to create a giant snowball? Pack it in a flat field? Okay, this works, but it certainly requires a large physical and mental expense. How about packing it atop a hill, which lies a few steps away? Harnessing the immediate passion that urges you to start this instant will set the base of success. The snowball will start small and behind pace of the immediate start. As time moves forward, the snowball will grow at a healthy rate, picking up size and momentum as it makes its way downhill. Looking over at the flat field version, it now lies in pieces, abandoned for the next big idea.

Next time you are filled with passion and a desire to create change, remember to take steps towards your dream, not leaps.

A journey of a thousand miles begins with one step. - Lao Tzu

Mentality

I've been doing it the same way for a long time and it has always "worked". It's just bad luck, things will come around. If we are doing the same thing as everyone else then we are going to be falling onto the same line of the Happiness U shape as everyone else. We need to think differently.

Broken Record Syndrome #LTESbrs

Now that we are armed with our weapon of mass change, small daily action, where do we target it? It can be very hard to see the forest through the trees as they say or, find where we need to fix things in our own life since we are too close to the matters to truly see them. Herein we find my method called the broken record syndrome. Broken Record Syndrome (BRS) is recurring patterns of speech targeted at life improvements, those of which are never followed through on, only wished upon.

Life Would Be Better If I Only…

BRS is a habit of inaction we fall into. I should start doing this. I should stop doing that. It is a continual desire to create change to live a happier more fulfilling life, followed up with nothing more than repeat thoughts. A desire creeps into our mind while we lie on the couch, sit in a cubicle, or operate in another routine life situation. What now? Door #1: Pat yourself on the back for the thought and take the comfortable route of doing nothing? Or, door #2: harness the idea and follow up on a potentially life enhancing change?

Door #1 or Door #2?

I could get up off the couch and take the first step toward my desire, or I could hit the snooze button on my life and lounge back down for just 10 minutes more. Which decision would you choose? Which decision should you choose? I know I certainly lean towards the latter, and do at times take door #2 and lie back down. We can all remember a time in our not-so-distant pasts when we thought of a really good idea and then shortly after rejected it for excess effort. My challenge to you is to not think of yourself at that instant. Instead, place yourself a day, week or year into your future and ask the question: "Are the decisions I am making now creating self-fulfillment and happiness in the future?"

Put It to Paper or Phone a Friend

Having trouble determining or remembering when you are afflicted with BRS? Write your symptom down on paper every time you catch yourself sounding like a broken record. Not sure if you suffer from BRS? Ask your friends, they will certainly diagnose you. After this, challenge them and hold each other accountable for creating happier, more fulfilling lives the steps—not leaps—way.

69

Maybe, Try, Next Week #LTESforbidden

Xiang Yiu in 207 BC had his army's ships burned to the ground to produce only one option. That option was no other choice but to push forward—retreat was no option. The night was spent on the beach, and upon waking in the morning, they realized they were under attack. The ships of theirs in the bay were on fire and burning down. The stark realization fell when they realized it was their own general who had burned the ships to the ground. He wanted his men fighting with desire and only one option on their minds. That was the path ahead with nothing behind. They fought under the knowledge of no retreat.

When we get into situations and start thinking of the road ahead, we begin to weigh our options. Now we don't have boats and armies at our disposal per se; however, our minds do have many resources and at their disposal that provide us with alternatives A-Z. Behind the workings of our mind is an area we will leave to psychologists to understand. For us, however, we have a few very valuable clues on the outside we can be searching for. The clues come in the form of what I will refer to as alternate-ending words. A very distinct path lays ahead, one that lacks clarity and thought. Instead of thinking harder into the subject, alternate-ending words pop up, doing nothing but delaying the decision into the future. These are words that conveniently slip out after our subconscious has told us that now is not the time to be addressing the topic at hand.

Who are the perpetrators alongside the subconscious? Maybe, Try and Next Week are the primary suspects. These words come into play when we are hitting a real tough spot and our brains are working too hard to come up with a path forward. All the sudden, an emotional easing is provided by simply putting it off until the future. We use these words to paint the path of emotional ease, thinking, "Well, I know it could not work out so I will mentally allow this as okay." Our friend Doubt is born when we start to accept these words and too much into our lives. This drops our dedication to the task as we take on way too many maybes and tries in our lives, only giving partial attempts to many things that have lower emotional value to us. Completing everything on our plate becomes nearly impossible without dedicating all of our time to tasks. Having more to do on our plates is not the answer. Doubt creeps into our mind all too often when we have to abandon tasks and do not follow through.

If the past is right—and it certainly has been in our minds—then we have all the reason in the world to doubt ourselves. We have had numerous things on our plate and many failed attempts. We dismiss aspirations and goals into the hands of our future-selves, in the hope we will be in a better place to take them on then. I will have extra time coming up, maybe I will start reading again. That is way over my head, I guess I could try, I can always give up, right? I don't have the time, maybe next week I will get to it. How about those picnic baskets and snares we can lay for our future selves, which category would these words fall under? Dismissing decisions to our future in hopes we will be able to deal with tough decisions then, SNARE. Let's start a list of troublesome words to look out for in our day to day conversation.

Maybe

Maybe I will start reading this weekend. Maybe I will get outside and go explore a new area. Maybe I will get back into painting. Whatever it is you are thinking of doing, it certainly holds some sort of value to you and would be meaningful to start or finish. However, attaching the parasitic maybe to it devalues the thought. We get a great feeling of what could be done and then immediately dismiss it to the land of our past attempts, where it just does not happen. Next time you catch this mischievous M word come out, examine the thought. Is this really worth doing? Will it provide fulfillment? If yes, then address the thought for what it is, and commit to leaving maybe at home. If the answer is no, then just forget about it!

Try

No one else is available, I guess I could try to do it. There is no way I will be able to do it, but I will try. Give me one more try. Try breaks down into two options – Option A, do it whole heartedly – Option B, accept a doomed try. It is clear option B is already accepted in our minds when this word arises. If in the event of completing the task whole heartedly (Option A) you falter, there will surely be valuable learnings for the next go around. When you catch this troublesome "t" word roll of your tongue prior to action, capture the thought and ask yourself if completing this task would leave you with a heightened sense of fulfillment. If yes, then do it without accepting option B.

Next week

Sounds like a great item for next week. Next week works better for me. Push it to next week, I won't be as busy. Are we delaying this item because we do not want to do it? Are we just feeling lazy right now? Is the task really worthwhile? Chances are, this extra bit of thought will iron the details out. Either the task is not worth your time, or it needs to be done. Ask yourself, is it really something I need to put off to next week or can I just do it now? Will next week actually be any better, or that just wishful thinking? Think past the small annoyance and embrace the fulfillment at the end of the task. If "next week" just slipped into the conversation, examine the idea and remember there will always be a next week but never another now.

Draw a great big circle on your wall at home and at the office (Sharpie or spray paint not recommended, but certainly an option). Slash a line through the middle and place these doubt laden words in the center. These words make their way into sentences when we haven't placed enough thought into the

74

situation. Examine the idea and either toss it, or fully engage the thought. As you go about your day, encourage others to hold you accountable to your big circle-slash thing. Think of it as the swear jar for progression. No more maybe trying next week—only get to what matters most now. Make sure to tell others of your bad habits and your effort to succeed. Urge them to do the same, and you will keep them up to speed. The power of community is described further in the last section of the book.

Faith and Hope #LTESfaith

From the journey of writing this book and looking to dissect what makes some people more prone to having smiles in their lives, a common thread to their happiness and fulfillment has always appeared. This common thread is faith paired with ever-increasing self-worth. This faith is not in the religious sense but faith in a better life being ahead. Self-worth develops from having faith that the actions we are taking right now are the right ones. Through this process of continued actions pertaining to our faith in a better self, comes building self-worth. This faith ties in with a muddy vision or mission of the path forward; those who tell you there is a very clear path should be taken with a grain of salt. Look at where you are now, was there a clear defined path to where you are now five years ago? Chat with someone who wears a smile wherever they go, someone in your network who is the epitome of fulfilled and happy. Was there a clear path for them? Probably not. Nothing is crystal clear, and when it comes down to it, life is an open system full of outside influence, which means we will never be able to predict things with full certainty.

When we wait for information to come along to take us from 80-100% certainty, it typically never comes, and it leaves us much further behind than if we were to just take that leap of "faith". The zero risk bias is one that continually holds us back from really great things in life. Daniel Kahneman takes a much more detailed look at this concept in his book Thinking for a Change (it is a heavier read but well worth it). The example he uses is companies who looked at buying out court cases involved with injury payouts. The individuals had very high certainty on winning cases (>95) that had a very high payout; however, nothing could be guaranteed and the weight of losing quickly consumes the mind with what-ifs. In steps a company that will pay you to take your winnings from the case, at a discounted payout for you, of course, but with a guarantee. The company assumes the liability in the case, which statistically is golden and you get a whole pile of money anyway at a discounted cut. This raises the question, if a company is willing to build its entire model around the consistency in our decision-making, how applicable is it to us?

Alright enough reading. Google double rainbow train (each one of us should get this excited in a day)

Now what do we need to have faith in, and how do we get this away from hope? Faith is the belief in a better self that is strengthened by our daily systems. Remove daily systems from this and we end up in the world of hope. Hope in this equation is a vision of our better selves, but with no daily routines or plan to move towards the end goal.

Super gigantic generalities are the main ingredient of hope. Hope takes the form for many of us as I hope to have more money, I hope to have more time and I hope then I will have no more problems. These out-there end goals come from not thinking deeply into what we would like to achieve and what it would mean to us. I hope to be richer one day. Well why? What would richer make you? Happier? Okay, what does happy look like? Scrooge McDuck diving into a sea of coins? What dollar figure do you need to make this happen? 10 million. Well, why 10 million? Because that could buy a big house and a maid to clean the rooms that never get used? We need to start asking ourselves these questions in order to develop honed in generalities. Otherwise, we will never connect the mission to now and autopilot life is still in control. As soon as we can create strong emotional ties to what we would like to achieve we will start to find something worth working towards. I need 1 million dollars to help feed 500 families a year for 10 years. The emotional tie is one that is very large and worth working towards, feeding 500 families. Granted we would then chop this big leap up into smaller chunks to take on. Perhaps your dream is to have 500,000 to pay off and rent a home here in order to travel the world with your kids and show them the wonders of what is out there. There is substance to this and it brings the meaning required to start building the actions to the mission. Otherwise generalities will rule, panic will flood in, and nothing will get done. This is the same mentality of, "I have 1000 things I need to do to be a better person." It is so mentally burdening that we get stuck in a state of inaction.

One thing we can see and imagine and feel is a better version of ourselves. This version lies in the now and in the future. Perhaps where you want to be in five years is on the side of a lake with a home that is routinely enjoyed with family. This is very clear, not just somewhere better than now with more money. That is far too general and not something to actively work to. It is important our subconscious is aware of these clear goals. If the subconscious is clear then it will provide the clarity to our decision-making on the conscious layer. Supercharge this vision with setting dates along the way; things become a lot more real when they close in on us.

This is where faith connects to a journey (who the heck knows exactly how to get there) and a mission: getting from point A to point B. Chris Guillebau brings clarity to this statement and has dedicated a blog and book (The Happiness of Pursuit) to it, I highly recommend both. Chris takes an angle and shines the light on missions. He starts with Christopher Columbus circumnavigating the world all the way to modern day video games and quests. His quest was to set foot through every country in the world, which he did in 11 years. Chris experienced the joy of setting a very specific end result, visited all the countries in the world, and figured out his path on the way along. The important part here is he did not set out with an absolutely concrete path, but he did set out with a concrete end.

Video games have taken such a heavy role in the life of many children and adults. They have also provided very lucrative and fulfilling lives for some. Where does the addiction in a video game come from? Why do some chase so hard for just one more? People love the feeling of accomplishment and growth that comes from levelling up. Why not take this perspective over to life? Have faith in becoming a better person, a higher level you and actively pursue this. The difference between this pursuit and hoping to become better, or hoping one day to wake up as a elf warlord, or something like that, is that one contains a belief of the endpoint and an active approach to getting there through levelling up. When we take this pursuit into our lives we begin to act with determination towards a specific end point. This determination and motivation shines through inspiring others, and the energy becomes contagious. It is much easier and much more likely at this point to attract those who are very like ourselves. We attract those who compliment our skills; no different than in a video game, our circle of influence grows and we attract like minded individuals. No one person has all the skills required to progress, and this is where a team becomes vital and enabled. In writing this book I did not put the launch plan together myself, I did not make the cover, I did not print the book, and many more aspects. I needed assistance and skills in others who shared my passion. That was one of the most important aspects of picking those to join me in my quest, they had to feel merit and be passionate about the journey.

Do not take the lottery approach to life and hope to fast track life with one swift jump. Identify the specific place you want to be, experience the emotions using creative thinking and visualization, and most of all have faith in yourself and your emotional ties to your mission. Start out on your mission tomorrow like a character in a video game strolling out on the first mission to a better self. Elf warlord or Kim Kardashian look alike?

Holes and Mountains #LTESbadDay

The journey has started. Every journey has holes to stumble and become lost in and also mountains where everything is clear and confidence is beaming. Do you ever have those days where you feel like nothing else could possibly go wrong? Bad luck followed by worse luck sends you deeper and deeper into a hole. If only a remote existed like Adam Sandler's Click, a simple squeeze of the fast forward button and voila! A new day in the form of tomorrow presents itself. We hope we won't fall into a rut, and maybe we will even be on top of a mountain.

Dark Clouds in The Forecast

You roll out of bed and your thoughts immediately turn. A feeling deep down inside warns of the rough day ahead. Perhaps the alarm has not rung and you are late for a big meeting. Perhaps you pour your cereal to find out you have no milk. Perhaps rain clouds roll in on your outdoor day that was planned. What else could possibly turn for the worse on this day? Everything. We will have days that do not go as planned. Alongside this fact, we can also find negatives in every aspect of our day if we search hard enough. With each new negative uncovered, we dig a deeper and deeper hole in our day and the days of those around us.

Life Across the Street

Complaining to others provides relief in the form of a sound-board. I am having the worst day ever for reasons A, B, and C. We hope for an affirmation in the form of "Wow, that day really does sound awful Calvin, you have all the right to be down." All of a sudden, a slap from reality hits us, and we learn that our complaints are really minor in comparison to that of our neighbours. There will always be someone in a worse place than you with a bigger smile on their face. From losing loved ones, to serious ailments, to financial troubles, we face numerous reasons to fill our head with woes. Cherish the ones you are still with, be thankful for the abilities you still have, and examine the happiness you have without a price tag in life. By adding up the positives, we build mountains for ourselves and those around us.

You have the ability to turn your day around at anytime without resetting to a new day. Next time you feel yourself heading into a hole, reframe the mounting negatives in your life and identify the positives. Spill your coffee on your pants or step in a foot deep puddle? Celebrate the low and appreciate the other side of your day when your foot wasn't in a puddle. One day I remember well was a Thursday in mid 2015. I woke up in the morning, was able to pry myself out of bed more easily than usual, and in the shower my brain kicked into gear, putting together the day ahead for me nicely. I threw on my set-out clothes, grabbed a bite to eat from the fridge, and was out the door with a spring in my step. Two steps across the hall

84

and I was ready to bound down the stairs of my apartment. Flinging open the door, I stepped into a puddle. Looking down to diagnose the situation, I saw a bunch of water and a blue collared golf shirt. Now out of all the routine mornings, this was by no means in any way close to normal, and all I could think was, "Why is there a golf shirt in a puddle in the stairway, and what is that brown pile beside...No. It can't be..." Now my mind started to race, is that dog... Human... Kaboom! The smell hits me in the nose, and I suddenly have no more desire to be Sherlock Holmes. Stumbling down the stairs at the speed of "almost going to puke Calvin" my mind raced with confusion—talk about a start to the day.

Getting outside now, I couldn't help but think what an awful start to this day, and then the thought crossed my mind. Could this day get any worse? The typical response to this sort of happening in a day is to get completely absorbed in self-pity. What a terrible day, all these other people out in the world are so much better off today, I hope everyone comes and gives me a hug and feels as bad for me as I feel for myself! I could have easily adopted this mindset, like I have many times before, but this time was different. Instead of being worried, I laughed. I just stepped in a puddle of yellow stuff, beside a pile of brown stuff. How could this day get worse? Pushing the scenario further, I imagined walking to work and being super soaked by a puddle full of street run-off behind the homeless shelter. Perhaps I would get to work, walk over to the fridge, saying hi to everyone along the way. With a skip in my step, I realize that after saying hi to the whole office that I have arrived to work with no pants on... As these scenarios started crossing my mind I thought back to what I just went through. What if I had slipped in the puddle and flopped right onto my back in it? Things certainly could have been much worse, although I almost feel like that would have been the best thing to happen. Like that super cold that comes along once every five years, this surely would have been my bad luck reset.

The lesson here is to not get caught up in the terrible day you are having. Instead, laugh at this anomaly, and dream up something funny that could make it worse. It is all too easy to judge our gutter days and be hung up on them.

Bad News or Just the Motivation You Needed #LTESkickInThe

You hate walking through the door at work, yet you dread losing the job. You have a significant other who does nothing but bring you down, yet you fear things will be worse without them. Have you ever received large scale news you dreaded, but secretly desired? Change most others would console you for however, oddly you did not feel sad, in fact a feeling of liberation rushed through you. It made your day, if not week, if not year.

The Flame That Never Extinguishes

Did a horrible boss fire you, or did you get laid off from a company that did not fuel your personal desires? Did a girlfriend or boyfriend just not fit and end it with you? When we are not feeling fulfilled in life, our inner person knows it, but our outward-acting individual is frightened of the change and discomfort. The two little voices are on each shoulder competing for your attention and toying with your desires. So often does our quick, outward-acting person suppress our subconscious, but the desire within is rarely extinguished. It holds strong.

We fear the inevitable result, but when the time comes and we finally follow our subconscious's lead and make the change, a feeling of gratification surges. As this feeling is identified we must ask ourselves the question, "Can we save ourselves this time and anguish, thwarting the unhappiness before it accumulates?" Yes, yes we can. In its simplest form, we must recognize the fact that we are not as happy as we can be. I am in no way saying drop everything at the first inclination of lesser feelings. Identify key recurring situations that lead to a decline in happiness or disengagement. These may include complaining about recurring events, counting down the hours till the end of the day, recurring daydreams of a better life. These are all situations which should pique your interest to create change.

Research from Stumbling Upon Happiness shows that we have a very, very poor ability to forecast the ability to add smile to our lives. The example that was used here was surveying engaged couples about the magnitude of having their significant other not show up on their wedding day. Hung out to dry at the church! Not so surprisingly, this was seen as the worst day that could happen in their life. No real surprise here. What was failed to take into account was how life would change after the event, which includes factors other than the sheer embarrassment and shock of not having the love of their lives show up. We have the distinct ability to only focus on specifics and not actually weigh in other factors such as how life could improve without the person in their life. Surely, if this were to happen, there were holes in the relationship on both ends.

However, for those who have been through this tragic experience, nearly all rated it as the best thing that had happened in their lives. This is a stark difference from the initial forecast. It turns out that life was not all about the loss of that day; we forgot to imagine how our lives might improve after that single moment. Have you had one of these moments in life? Whether it be a breakup, job loss, or other life event, seemingly it was the worst thing that could happen yet when you come out the other side it was the best thing to happen?

When on vacation in a beautiful place you continually hear people with big smiles on their face saying, "One day I just decided to do it, there were no more excuses left, and I have never been happier since."

Do not accept merely existing on this planet. Embrace living. Abolish perceived barriers; chase your desire even though the path ahead may not be entirely clear. Some say this is an attitude bred from impulse, but I believe this attitude is driven from a developed intuition and desire.

Planning Your Funeral #LTESfuneral

Here's a little assistance from your future self to get you moving today. I am currently planning my funeral, not because I see the end near, but because I want to better understand the life I have yet to live and what I would like to accomplish and be remembered for. For my 26th birthday, I will actually be sitting down with friends and family to bring appreciation and realization to the time we have left together by planning each of our funerals. When it comes down to it, this is all we really have. I spent two very impactful hours sitting down with Ben Calica, a very passionate advocate of living a life of legacy. Ben helps families understand and plan for the passing of a life. The basis of this planning is not that you are on your deathbed now, but far from it. The overarching question to be addressed and planned out is, what legacy would you like to leave? In addressing this question and actively working towards the answer, a life of legacy can be created every single day.

What legacy will you leave?

How do you want to be remembered over your lifetime? This can be a legacy of a loving and caring parent with a life dedicated to their children. This could be a life dedicated to creating change in this world. Some will most be interested in leaving the world in better shape than when they entered it. Personally, I will leave a legacy of helping others to increase their happiness and realize their best selves.

Who will be at your funeral?

These will be people you already know and people you have not met yet. We have certainly had an impact on many people in our lives up until now, so these individuals will be fairly easy to place into the picture. The real thinking here comes when we plan for those we have not yet met. What sort of characteristics do these people have? How were they drawn to us and how were we drawn to them? My family and all those with whom I have had the pleasure of sharing a laugh are front and center in my mental image. Those in the back, who I have not yet met, are all pursuing a life rich with smiles and helping others.

What pictures will be up?

What single picture will you be remembered by in the paper? What pictures will your friends and family bring to commemorate you? What emotions will you be showing in these pictures, and which events in your life brought these emotions forward? For myself, I see a picture taken at a family event relaxing and laughing at the very top. Other photos will be from around the world with close friends. Some of the biggest smiles I have in photos are from when I was exploring the beauty of the world.

Instead of burying our heads in the sand at the distant fact of our own funeral, let's accept this event with open arms and plan the legacy of our best possible selves.

Vacation Memory #LTESexperience

What is this journey and life legacy without memories of the great time had? Life through the eyes of Instagram? I continually find myself leaning to my calendar, social media and my pictures to remember what happened in a week. This for many is becoming the norm; our cell phones live so close to our sides that if we need to remember something, we just take a picture. This has added benefits of offloading some of the power necessary to remember things, freeing up time for the brain to perform other activities such as which hashtag to use! When it comes to life and the very end, our years can be summed up from the memories we retain. When we proceed through life with no memories and nothing really new, the turbo boosters hit. Seven years go past and we can find ourselves wondering what happened. What were the highlights of your 2015? How about 2016? Does it seem that this year is almost half over and not much memorable has happened? Now, I want you to place yourself in the shoes of your last vacation, how well can you remember your days? I am guessing your vacation memory is much better than your memory for the last week or even two weeks prior. Why would this be? Vacation is a world full of new experiences, getting out there into a new environment full of new actions and decisions, where you are actively looking to experience new situations.

Joshua Foer tells it well of the powers our imagination can unlock in ourselves if we simply restart this long abandoned trait from our childhood, the power to imagine. Imagination is the power to immerse ourselves in the moment so as to remember it for as long as possible. Take a break from the cell phone and actually soak in your surroundings. When was the last time you paused to listen, smell, taste, view, and touch your surroundings? I mean really truly pause to soak it all in, to the utmost of your capabilities? This is experience at its peak. Take a moment now to feel this book or e-reader. Feel the texture of the object, the temperature, the weight as it extends from your fingertips to your arms and into your body. What sounds are currently around you? Think hard to what has become routine, perhaps a dull hum from a computer or the tick from a clock. What smell is in the air? If there is nothing noticeable, try lighting a candle or smell your hands. Yes, I just said smell your hands. What thought does the smell in the air remind you of? Where does it take your imagination? Coming back now, take a few deep breaths. Feel your chest rise and fall. What do you taste? Finally, what colors are around you? Observe from the corners of the walls all the way down to the floor from side to side. Set a calendar event tomorrow at a random time that simply says experience. When it reminds you, pause. Listen, smell, taste, view and touch your surroundings. Step forward into experiencing situations fully; remove the reliance on your phone and pictures for memory. It all starts with our minds and our ability to think back and re-create the wonderful moments from our past.

You will relearn the ability to slow down time in your life as you re-learn the ability to imagine and experience. Tests have been run on those with the best memory in the world, and their brains are no different than ours. The difference is which part of the brain is activated when someone actively remembers an object, the visual memory. Try and remember the first home you lived in when you were a child. How did it look? Take some time to paint the picture and now think of how you remembered it. Do this from a visual perspective, not by the usual technique we now use to remember, which is repetition. I highly recommend Moonwalking with Einstein for a much more detailed approach to using your visual memory to become one of the world's best.

Along with the distinct ability to remember comes a distinct ability to improve our emotional state in the moment. Wouldn't this be beneficial? You can go in 2 minutes or less from weak and dull, to strong and energetic. No, you do not have to buy a magic pill. We all have these states in us, we just need to find them. In combining the laboratory work of Amy Cuddy and Paul Ekman, we have our gateway to on-demand discovery.

Amy is a social psychologist who is well known for her TED talk covering power poses and the effect these poses have on the hormones cortisol and testosterone in our bodies. Testosterone is the hormone associated with dominance, and cortisol with stress. In the world of primates, the alpha males are found to have higher levels of testosterone and lower levels of cortisol. This has also been found in powerful leaders, male or female. The specific laboratory tests boil down to taking on low power poses, which are generally associated with taking up less room, and high power poses characterized by taking up space. These poses were held for 2 minutes and then the attendant's hormone levels were compared to their baseline, which was established earlier. In the high power poses, 20% increases in testosterone and 15% decreases in cortisol from baseline were experienced. In low power poses, 10% decreases in testosterone and 25% Increases in cortisol from baseline were experienced.

Paul is a psychologist who has dedicated his life's research to emotions and our facial expressions. One of the many tests Paul has performed is to have a subject mentally visualize times of peaked emotional state from the past. For two minutes, subjects transported themselves back to a time of heightened happiness, sadness, or another definitive emotion. What Paul found was the same emotional responses that were experienced at the specific time in the past were brought up again. Physical posture changed, subjective feelings, and even facial expressions adopted dominant characteristics of the associated memories. I highly recommend his book Emotions Revealed if any of this is of interest. Digging a bit deeper into nice-to-know realm, it is possible to go back into a memory and change it. Think about a time you were really angry at someone and a grudge stuck, then finally you talked to them about it and realized why they did what they did. This realization provides ease and understanding in the memory to change the associated feelings.

Tying these two findings together, we find our solution to changing the emotions we are experiencing at any given time. Of course depending on the severity of the emotion being experienced this will not be as easy. However, when going through our day at work, this typically is not the case, and by adopting these two approaches you will be able to see large changes in your ability to control emotion at just the right time—whether it be for a big meeting, on a day you are just feeling off, or perhaps for a job interview. Try out power posing while remembering a time of heightened power or joy in your past. The quickest way to an emotional state change is to lead with your physical presence. Pairing this with a memory of the past, one that shares the emotional state you are searching for, is the key to fast, effective changes.

Remember a time of intense happiness and relive the emotion. The easiest go-to here is time with family. Do you have kids? Think of the joy they bring you daily, and it will be nearly impossible to feel mad. What do you find beauty and raw emotion in? This is what you are searching to remember and harness in your life. Pair this with a power pose, and you have a recipe to generate positive emotions on demand. Try it now: find a strong power posture of yours and visualize a time in the past of extreme happiness and joy. Nightly journaling where you record your positive thoughts can help here. Spend time at the end of your day to reflect backwards on the best parts of your day. Write these events down emotionally. If you had a blast, make sure you hit the trigger of why you had a blast. If Becky spit water through her nose, write down the pre-events from the simple conversation, to the building laughter, all the way through until the good-looking guy saw her spit water out of her nose. And of course, don't forget the laugh you had as you witnessed this and the evil eye you received in return. Reflect back on these moments when you are having a tough day, or just review them every week to get you into a good mood.

Toast to the Future #LTEStoast

Having faith in your better self and your ability to visualize the future brings us to the next step: celebrating what is in our future. I was recently sitting in a coffee shop and overheard a toast from two ladies, both later into their lives: "Cheers to the future." Such a simple statement yet so full of meaning.

All the Best Years Have Gone By

So often when we hit a milestone age, we reflect backwards and think, "Wow, those times were sure amazing, they certainly cannot be matched in the future." Reminiscent memories of the past dominate mind, leaving joy and happiness in the dust, alongside our best years.

Energy Direction

Which do we have control over, setting direction in our past or our future? Where is it best to spend more time and energy, dwelling on the past, or creating our future? Yes, these are loaded questions. Next time a worrying situation from our past comes to mind, let's take on the challenge of reframing the thought. How can we create a better future learning from the valuable mistake in our past? What action can we take to assure success going forward? As Rafiki put it long ago [with my substitution], "The past can hurt, but the way I see it, you can run from it [dwell on it] or, learn from it."

Let's not create the life we think we want 20 years from now. Instead of waiting, let's take action to improve immediately. Engaging in these first steps will create the momentum for a happier, more fulfilling life each and every day, week, and year.

Time—what an interesting and mentally challenging aspect of our lives. It feels like we have all the time in the world in some moments; then in others it is like there is none remaining. Often I find myself wishing for more time in my life to get things done. Then when I look at what more time would get me, it turns out to look a lot like what I am doing now and not really getting me anywhere. Herein lies a massive challenge. What should I be spending time on, and what should I really be dropping? In reality, not everything is deserving of my time and adopting an attitude closer to "hell yeah!" or "no" helps with this conundrum. Toast to the "hell yeahs" upcoming in your life, and move forward with faith in creating the better version of yourself. We cannot change the past, but we sure can change the future. Next time you raise a glass, make a toast to your future.

Path Forward

I was going to do something today that could have been life changing, but then I thought about failing and decided it would be easier to just not start.

Brain Wiring #LTESredbull

I have a faulty piece of equipment up top—it doesn't work like everyone else claims theirs does. My brain thinks what is good for me is actually bad, and what is bad for me, is actually good. I can't help but think Calvin+ and Calvin- are crossed.

Worst Case Scenario

The struggle between what is good for us and what is actually detrimental rages on everyday. A task gnaws at us for the longest time, and our subconscious pushes it to the surface. Each time it comes up as a meaningful item, and each time it is observed in the worst case scenario and banished by our conscious back into the depths of our mind. The next time you think you find yourself in this predicament, question yourself – Is it truly bad, or am I just dismissing the idea for the worst case?

Ditch the Red Bull, Take Up The Wish List

Wake up in the morning, struggle through the first moments (brushing my teeth is the tipping point for me) and get to a pad of paper. Write down that one thing you have dreaded to do, the one thing that has been on your mind all week, month, or even year. Slip it into your pocket and face it all day. Take the task on and experience the energy surge as you cross it off; the feeling will far surpass any pick me up a Red Bull could induce. Fail to get it done and learn from the day, whether you were just too busy or perhaps you were in need of a bigger nudge. Take away the learnings, and slip the paper in your pocket another day.

All too often we visualize the worst-case scenario and nothing else. No wonder we don't want to step into meaningful tasks. Thinking about completing this article, I would have most likely been hit by a car on the way to the coffee shop, frozen up writing, posted the article on LinkedIn and been ridiculed by all my connections. I know at least two of these did not happen, which means worst-case scenario averted. Grab a piece of paper, write down one of those items from the depths of the to-do list, slip it into your pocket, and re-verse the crossed wiring.

What is the best way to learn? Reinvent the wheel, and re-learn the path that so many have plowed in front of us? Certainly not, by this time we are on the right path of learning from others; however, here is where we find another mental limiter that is holding us from moving forward: the belief that we cannot learn from everyone we cross in our day.

VP of the World #LTESgardening

Wow, with a title like that I bet that person could really help me out with a few questions, but they are out of my league. Maybe someday I can have a chat with them. Wow, I wonder what it is like to be as low as that person in life? I will never be there, I am glad to be out of that league. Where does quality conversation stem from, having the same titles on business cards? The brand of car you drive? The neighbourhood you live in? Sure, these all might be conversation starters, but true meaningful conversation comes from deeper within. It evokes our shared values, interests, and an understanding that we all have differing journeys.

Barriers

Why don't we feel like we can have meaningful conversations with those around us? We place false barriers in our own heads that restrict us from meaningful connections. False barriers leave those at the top feeling very lonely, and they prevent those seemingly below us from sharing valuable life lessons. I have been around numerous technical professionals who have passed this story along to me – "We were having such a great conversation before my name was announced to present, but after returning from the stage, the conversation ended. The individual on the other side seemed too humbled by the perception of elevated knowledge to carry on the chat following the presentation." On the flip side, I have, and I am sure you have, dismissed someone's value by their appearance. This can happen as you pass by on the street and think, "What a hippy," or "That person certainly must be homeless." Many times, these thoughts are followed up by a humbling conversation or discovery. Barriers are placed all too easily, and we are prone to dismissing opportunities prior to any meaningful interaction.

The Gardener

A defining moment I had, when I realized we are all people at the core, came at a recent technical conference. After a full two days of technical content, no one was outwardly interested in talking any more technicalities; however, it stayed the default. Changing the conversation from technical content to "What do you enjoy outside of work?" sparked conversation like no one experienced that day. It looked like a world of weight had been lifted from this individual's shoulders and the response came: "Gardening. I wish I could spend more time gardening these days, it is where my passion lies." After the many decorated years, this subject matter expert has been dreaming of the simple task of gardening. After a mental walk through the magnificent garden at home, we had developed a bond far surpassing any work-related, technical bridge that was possible. A quality connection arises from learning what makes an individual unique.

The Best Quesadilla in Town

While spending time in a foreign city recently, I had ventured out of the center and sparked up conversation with a man most would not have. He had a rough exterior, and most passing turned their heads down, not willing to have the simplest of conversation. He asked me, "Do you have change to spare for food?"

"Why yes I do, I am however looking for Quesadilla recommendations, any advice? And, would you be interested?" I said.

"Certainly, I know a spot just a few blocks away," he answered. This proved to be the most memorable of interactions, and one of the tastiest quesadilla experiences to date.

I am not saying that you will only learn new food spots from those perceived to be lower than you and gardening tips from experts. However, there is value in conversation with all types of people you encounter. You just need to explore meaningful conversation, leveling the field with neither talking down, nor up. We all view the world through a different lens; it is neither better nor worse, only different.

Pass the Salt #LTESlenses

When having conversation with more and more people with diverse backgrounds and opinions, you must learn how to filter this information. Long ago said to be an antidote to poisons, we now use the saying in everyday conversation when we are skeptical of the sentences, or more aptly, the stories constructed by others: "Take it with a grain of salt." We have certainly had these words sent meaningfully our way in the past. Should we heed this advice? Or should we soak up the initial conversation and continue on with our day?

Limitless Lenses

Like our mothers always told us, there are two sides to any story, and we better hear them both before we construct our version. Think back to a time when you and someone else have been asked to retell an event you both experienced firsthand. Both stories start, the major details are more or less consistent, but then the minor details and filler are very much askew. Why is it when two people see the same thing they recall it differently later? We all have the same information coming in to our eyes; however, we each have a filter that is applied, and we process and store the information differently. We all view the world through different lenses, just like we each have on our own pair of glasses. Hence, no one story is naturally retold the same way by two people.

Your View of the World

We are continuously subjected to alternative opinions and viewpoints throughout our day. How then do we shape our own view of the world? Surely we know it is best to not believe everything we hear during our day, yet at the same time, we cannot discredit all that enters our eyes and ears. When constructing our view of the world, remember we all have individual biases born from past experience. Try to understand the viewpoints and perspectives from the diverse backgrounds and histories of the individuals you speak with. From old to young, high salaries to low wages, European to North American, we all have diverse backgrounds and understandings of the world around us. Shape your view of the world through a combination of those around you.

Take all of your casual conversations with a grain of salt and be open to conversation from all types of people, as we can truly learn something from everyone. Do not completely discount—or blindly agree—with those who you are locked into conversation with. Develop an understanding of the other person's perspective and shape your viewpoint using the wisdom of combined thinking. It is not negative to take everything you hear with a grain of salt; it is realistic. Oh, and remember what your face looks like when you are soaking in the conversation. The face of skepticism is not a pretty one.

The Green Ball/ Spider in Amazon #LTESfavsoup

When was the last time you purchased a new vehicle? Surely before turning your interest to this purchase, you almost never saw the same vehicle on the road. Now that you have purchased the vehicle, every single person went out and bought the same vehicle on the same day! What were the chances? How about that time you entered the creepy bathroom in the woods? Sitting down, you quickly and thoroughly scanned every single corner, fearing the giant nasty spider. Only to find... a big nasty spider!

These are examples of how our mind filters and prioritizes information in our minds. Stop and listen for a minute. Do you hear any annoying sounds in the room? Where is it coming from and why did you not hear it before? It is like the amplitude is now cranked and that is all the mind can focus on. This is a filter our mind puts up, sorting for information to solidify information we seek. This filter is usually put up in a situation that requires an element of focus in our life such as, say, in our caveman years when we were walking through the bush shopping for blueberries and stumbled upon a friendly bear coming off of a red meat fast. Let's say we are also hungry and heading over to the blueberry patch. A stomach grumbling keeps us determined to walk past the beautiful flowing river and magpies chirping along in the trees without noticing them. Honed in on our hunger is where we meet our bear friend who shares something in common, a hunger and focus on this hunger. Your husband is back in the cave and has given you a verbal laundry list of items to collect. Pick up some sticks, find some kindling, pick up some river rocks and on and on before, berries! Now walking out of the house your mind was stuck on berries and all else begins to fall away as the hunger grows and your filter strengthens for food. Alas, Hungry Harry the bear is in the same state at the berry patch, and unfortunately he still has a filter applied. This filter is locking him into a hunger focus, filtering for information that supports the primary focus. Now, you fall into sight of Hungry Harry as he licks his chops. Springing into action, unfortunately your name is now action, his eyes lock onto you and the berry patch is quickly forgotten. Your filter of food and hunger is now shocked into one of survival, the most important filter to you in the moment. The berries are suddenly feeling a tad lonely as your focus now changes away from them and onto dodging Hungry Harry. From the teeth and the speed of approach, to any obstacles in your way, to the advice you received from that oh so wise elder in the village called *National Geographic*. Do you play dead with black bears or grizzly bears, and what on earth is Harry the hungry bear? Suddenly not much else matters than the task your mind is focusing on, Hungry Harry!

Our minds have been conditioned for a very long time to address what is immediate, such as hunger, fear, sleep, and other states heavily determined by emotion. This focus is what has led us to many great things in life such as champion sports teams, dodging Hungry Harry, and the focus necessary to hone in on our food as it drops from the microwave allowing us to react just in time after it hits the floor and splashes everywhere. Bye bye broccoli soup (can you tell I am still bothered by it? #LTESFavSoup). This focus, like any super power, can be used for evil in our lives. When we get into snaps of anger, self-doubt, and negativity, what we choose to think about will take the lead spot in our minds.

Have you seen the Listerine commercials with the tooth brush and toothpaste gallivanting around solving the serious life problem of GINGIVITIS? If not, Google it prior to reading this next line because you will need to take on the voice of the actor in this commercial. No different than our brains focusing on the new car we purchased or that nasty spider in the jungle, it also filters for NEGATIVITY. Take yourself back to a rut in life. Did it not seem almost insurmountable? Moment after moment and day after day, it was almost as if the bad luck would never stop. This is the not so-nice-side of focus that we all have. This is the ability to worry ourselves sick and not see any good in our days, and it can become overwhelming.

There are many factors that affect our mood in a day and ability to maintain a positive demeanor. Some of the most influential are the maintenance of our bodies, our expectations of what we deserve, and lastly, the people we surround ourselves with. Losing sleep and poor diet have surely afflicted all of us. Without sleep, our minds do not repair, and thinking becomes impaired. Throw diet out the window, and with it goes our health. The dreaded expectation mindset, everything else comes so easily to others, yet little old me just can't catch a break. And the people. From bad relationships, to negative friends, all the way to toxic co-workers, maintaining a positive approach to the day gets sidetracked all too easily when we do not have the right people around us.

Emotional Mirroring and Refractory #LTESblind

Can you think of one person in your life who can find the worst out of any situation? How frustrated do you become when spending time with this person? How does it affect your outlook on the day? How about the flip side—think about someone in your life who can find the best in any situation. Now let's play a game of pick the friend you would like to spend more time with. Who provides more value to your life? As people, it becomes natural for us to mirror the attitudes of those around us. Try not smiling around someone who is cracking a grin from ear to ear. How about being around someone angry, just try to get into a good mood. How about a situation in your life where you wanted to be scared but the person beside you stayed confident, and this behavior somehow miraculously wore off on you?

Emotional Refractory Period

Our emotions. They are a wild and seemingly untameable beast at times. Throughout the spectrum of experience, we meet Sadness, Anger, Fear, Surprise, Disgust, Contempt, and Happiness. These are the core emotions researched by Paul Ekman through his novel Emotions Revealed and his hit show Lie To Me. In his research, Dr. Ekman discovered something called the emotional refractory period. The emotional refractory period is exactly what we experienced while running from Hungry Harry. Our mind locks in on what matters most and only that during heightened levels of emotion. It is like a supercharging of that specific emotion, providing a prolonged period of time here prior to returning to normal. This is very handy in situations where Hungry Harry may come back for round two. It is much less convenient when we get into an argument with our spouse, experience road rage, or endure a loss that feels like the pain will never go away.

Once our brain is stuck in an emotional state filter, it becomes very hard to remove ourselves. Ever made a decision you regretted? This is thanks to our emotional refractory period. Perhaps you should have just waited 24 hours before acting.

Pairing Dr. Ekman's research with some of Dan Gilbert's findings in Stumbling on Happiness, we find that we are no good at seeing ourselves in a state other than the one we are experiencing in the moment, for example, when you wake up tired in the morning and you are certain nothing in your day would possibly come between you and being in bed on time. Then along comes bedtime and you can't imagine how you felt in the morning and why you ever thought you should go to bed on time. In neither situation are we capable of feeling any other way than we do. Along comes being deep in love with someone and thinking the world will never be anything but roses and doves. Then 5 years go by and you couldn't ever imagine why you were with that person. Or when you lose a pet, the grief in the moment is insurmountable and thoughts of how you will ever survive run rampant. Yet a mere few months down the road, you discover a happy life is still possible.

The Importance of Progression
#LTESforward

What was the last thing you accomplished? When did you set your mind to something that was not in reach yet and put the work in to get there? The journey may have been long or short, but there was a definite journey from Point A to Point B. Think of Point A and the road you had ahead. What sort of emotions were you feeling? Perhaps some weariness at the end goal, or maybe you were confident in your abilities. Were you scared at the thought of failure? Were you scared at the thought of success? Remember the time and relive the emotion.

Now transport yourself to Point B. Re-experience what it felt like right when you reached that point. What was the feeling when you actually reached the goal, perhaps a rush of excitement and deep sense of pride? Maybe an odd sense of calm and satisfaction? Looking back on the journey, it can often be hard to know where the emotion or self-doubt ever came from. The growth experienced over this time will certainly have elements of failure, a plan or idea that was present and absolutely fell through. At the time it could have been difficult to fathom moving forward. However, you are at Point B now. You pushed through it and proved to yourself that it was possible. You progressed.

The importance of this story is not A. It is not B. It is all of the space starting before, spanning the middle, hitting B, and not stopping there. If we are not constantly progressing in our lives, we will never be as fulfilled as possible, whether it be in a relationship, career, or other interest. When we do not progress, we grow unhappy and dissatisfied.

When we keep our relationships exciting and new we progress in them. This progression in turns brings us more smiles in our lives. When we are not doing new things, we fall into a stale state and things get dull very quickly. In our careers, we often fall into ruts of no learning and little self-improvement. Also, think of the hobbies and interests in our lives. When we learn new skills that allow us to golf a better game, we are happier. When we learn a new knitting technique or find a new mentally stimulating book, we are on top of the world! Progression is also obtained through others. Watching those closest to us progress through their journeys in life can be one of the most rewarding experiences of all. Just ask a parent what makes them the happiest and most fulfilled in their days. Surely, it is being with their children and watching them progress.

Without all of the struggles and successes, we lead boring and unfulfilling lives. Think of yourself right now. How would you feel if your life did not change for one month, six months, five years, or 10 years? Think of yourself today and what it would be like if you were the same person as you were one month, six months, five years, or 10 years ago. We stack the smile odds against ourselves when we are not moving forward. Remember steps, not leaps when progressing in your life. Two of the most supercharged experiences I have had lately were buying a water bottle and taking jeans in to the repair store. Yes, these two very trivial things had a very high impact on me. I had put both these tasks off for about one year total. Thinking about doing them multiple times a week I had failed many, many times in getting such trivial things done. Put the book down now, and think about something that has been nagging you for a long time that is very easy to do. Can you do it now? If so, go do it. If not, do it at the next available time, and not like the next available time like I have given myself hundreds of times. Do it at the actual next time you can. It is now a high priority ☺.

In the words of a fellow author and friend Chris Spurvey, "Because people are at their best when they are moving toward something that they desire. These individuals have a burning desire to help people. They have a passion for life. But they also know that people are never happy when they are standing still. It is the anticipation of putting their all into something that makes people happy."

Prove Self-Worth #LTESsquared

Now that we know high intensity and long-term goals destine us for failure, we want to take the first steps toward constant progression in our lives. The focus now will be on low pain, small-duration progression (over and over). Through this process of small progress daily, we find the key to building happiness, which is building our self-worth.

30 day challenges run rampant today, whether it's hitting the gym for 30 days in a row, reading 30 pages for 30 days, or eating nothing but the finest of fresh for 30 days. Disclaimer: do not try these at home, or anywhere else in your life. There is a big problem with most people's views on 30 day challenges. That problem is people think they should be hard. The perception is that these challenges need to challenge our perfect self. This sets the bar way too high—in unrealistic realms—which only sets us up for failure, and in turn, diminishes self worth.

The squared method is a form of chunking and gamification that makes things manageable and encouraging for the entire duration. Placing goals for long periods of time becomes far too mentally tolling and unrealistic. Our subconscious knows this and with little to no light at the end of the tunnel, goals become easy to abandon. I want to transport you now to a situation: you're taking on a challenging pace up a set of very long stairs that zigs and zags up the side of a hill in nice short durations. Start at the bottom and do not take your eyes off of the top of the stairs. As you focus on the top your mind now begins to weigh your effort against that specific end point. It will not take long for your mind to take a hold of what you are attempting and put the brakes on the task to preserve you.

Now, let's try this again but this time with the approach of only looking to the end of the specific set you are on. With your focus on the top of each small set, the mental pain is much lesser. As you make your way up, mini celebrations start to occur with each small victory, spurring you on with little boosts each time. Both methods will only work up until your body and muscles tire out. The biggest limiter we are addressing here is our minds shutting us down, which will almost always come prior to our bodies shutting down. Our mind is the limiter here and for good reason. It is there to protect us. We can combat this by chunking up the entire goal into smaller, much more manageable pieces. This is an element of gamification.

Think of a game or a task that is spread out over a long duration. How motivated are you going to be if you have 200 hours ahead of you that will be dedicated to a task, say at work? Let's think of progress towards that goal. How exciting is it to see the goal approaching at a rate of 200, 199, or 198? Not very. Now what if we chunk up those 200 hours into mini goals of 10 hours, each with a defined endpoint. Say you are venturing across a nation. If you look only at the end result as being the highlight, everything along the way is painful. Instead, if you take the approach that each city you pass through is equally important and part of the journey to be celebrated, then the journey becomes much easier to take. Looking at each stopping point as progress is much more exciting than simply shooting for the end target.

At the core of gamification is our desire to compete, progress, and support others' growth. You will see online education as heavy utilisers of gamification to make learning much more fun and engaging, if not borderline addicting. Marketing is so often turned into a game to spur interaction; these are your "for a chance to win" contests. Share this update with 10 others and receive a free month trial. Collect 10 stamps or game board pieces and have a chance to win. Being a Canadian, our most well-known gamification product experience is roll up the rim to win eh. Every year Time Horton's brings out their famed prize cups, and the frenzy begins. It has actually become much less about the product and more about the win. At work, we hold contests to see who can come up with the best win-to-lose ratio. Many people who may drink one coffee per week get sucked into 3-4 coffees a week, all in the name of winning a potential prize.

What does this mean in the name of happiness and fulfillment? If life progression is no fun for you, then make it into a game. Now, there is no need to re-invent the wheel here. Think about the games in your life that are borderline addict-

ing or that you find a ton of fun. What are the core components of points, progress, and competition in the game? Ex-
periment with replicating these components in your life and
in your tasks. And what would a game be if you didn't have
someone to play with? Much less exciting, that is what! Life is
much more fun and motivating when sharing experiences
with others.

Perhaps you have a good friend who shares your interests that
you can take this game on with together. Sit down once per
week to review progress, and place a friendly bet on it. Who-
ever does not meet the goals set out for the week buys breakfast, coffee, etc. This is the game portion of the challenge, and
it is based in very short manageable intervals, which is key.
This game is cooperative, not good vs. evil. You are not pitted
against your friend and trying to lay down a crushing defeat
every week. Sure, it is great to laugh along at each other's mis-
steps. However, do not ever bring someone into your game of
life who is only interested in laughing at your mistakes and
not supporting your success. You are in this game together,
providing a helping hand in troublesome spots and reminding
each other that you are not only accountable to yourself but
someone else. You are not alone in this journey! You are com-
mitting task suicide by placing a span of one year on your
goals with a friend. You will never get it done and the game
would absolutely suck with only one opportunity per year for
reflection, point gain, and opportunity to celebrate. Now that
we have laid the value out for chunking up challenges into

small pieces and the basis behind setting realistic 30 day goals, we find ourselves at another component of gamification, visual aids.

Let's think about the visual aid in our life of a grocery list. We write down apples, carrots, spinach, pasta sauce, chicken breast, eggs, toothpaste, and bread on the list. How likely is it that we will not pick up everything on the list as it stares us in the face? Well, pretty unlikely, unless the chickens have rebelled and are now taking over the world. Now think about going back into the grocery store with no list in hand. How well do you do? Much worse. When we hold things in our minds, we set ourselves up for failure as our minds are continually running in circles, processing all of life's other challenges. We are no different with our 30 day challenge being held only in our minds. It seems like a great task for our perfect self; however, we know that to be nothing other than a phony now. Instead, we need to draw ourselves out 30 nice big squares in a high visibility spot. I like to have this one within reach during the start of the day as a reminder, like on the door before you leave the house. Five big old squares across and six down, filling in all that space for our 30 nice big empty squares. As each day goes by, we put an X in the square to mark it complete. If you are able to see yourself progressing along your task, you will become motivated to continue. If at any time you miss a day you have to restart at 0. Doing this brings in an element of accountability. This is accountability to your past self, as seen by progress, and accountability to your future self, as seen by the end game.

Remember make these things easy. I do not want to see anything harder than silencing your phone for two hours in a day. This is all about setting yourself up for success. When picking your task, it is also very important to remember and write down the other components. These components are the keys to your success and value to you.

The keys to success: What do you need to keep in mind everyday to ensure success? Think about thwarting your mind here. Planning for tasks such as cell phone silence, keep in mind times of the day you will not be able to silence your phone and avoid these. Say you have to be around your phone at work and you have phone calls later at night. Slot this time in to happen right after work and before the phone calls.

Value to you: What would it mean to you to complete these 30 days? Think emotionally here. If you could make it 30 days with cell phone breaks, how would that feel to you? Think of the mental clarity you gain in these hours and the freedom from expectation you are now gifting yourself.

A few squared challenges I have completed and highly recommend are no cell phone for two hours, morning physical activity, and cold water routines.

Silencing your phone for two hours: This allows us to get back into a realm of experience. It is all too easy for us to always be thinking of our phones now. Even if it is not in our hands we are constantly reminded by the bulge in our pocket of that little device that just may have a present for us in the form of a like, share, alert, mail or text. By dedicating a full two hours to no cell phone, we clear our headspace and open it up for things like experiencing our surroundings again. We don't have to wonder what is going on with our friends in social media, or what is happening at work through email, or just plain and simply, what is happening on the Internet. Shedding these thoughts leaves us scrambling for other thoughts to occupy our mind, conveniently setting ourselves up to experience more of our surroundings.

Morning physical activity: Try out a small amount of exercise right when you get up for 30 minutes a day. It is guaranteed that you will have to wake up every morning and do something, so insert 20 push-ups or a breathing routine to shock your body into morning action. This is a great approach to shed the morning haze and shed it fast.

On the topic now of morning haze, we find another morning routine that is common to many, showering. Blast yourself with uncomfortably cold water for 15 seconds every morning to shock your body into action and to shed that morning haze. Don't shower in the AM? Try washing your face with cold water for 30 days straight, and let me know the result.

As you pick your squared challenge try to pick mornings. They are a great place to target as it starts your day off with a victory. Things become a lot easier in a day when you have a small success within an hour of waking. Do not cheat yourself; it is only for 30 days, and if you have any inclination you may not have been true to the task, do not stick with it. This is about proving you can do it

Heavier Pockets #LTESdaily

Everyday we have the opportunity to make small positive changes in our waking hours. I am guessing most understand this and have even tried it out wholeheartedly, one small meaningful action a day. I know I have, and I have also completely fallen on my face two days in, due to a selective memory. This is where I have turned to paper and pockets to thwart my mind. Before stepping out of the door in the morning, I write a maximum of 5 words on a piece of paper and make it my happiness goal to complete for the day. As that paper burns a hole in my pocket, I can no longer dismiss the thought to the depths of my mind. Morning-Calvin holds rest-of-the-day-Calvin accountable for creating happiness in the short term, with the long term in mind.

In order to keep myself in line and targeted, I display a list of the categories I pull from below. I encourage you to stuff your pocket with one of the topics this week and add to the list as you go! Before you know it, you will be at 365 days of conscious happiness.

Reconnect with an Old Friend

Touch base with an old friend. Pick a family member, childhood friend, or a co-worker of the past and reach out to them. Reminisce over the times that were, and celebrate the times to come. Laugh about the good times, and empathize with each other about the bad times. Time goes by all too fast. In the moment, it is as if the feelings will never slip away and then POOF! Life happens. Take a moment to appreciate the people and moments of the past.

Kindness Ripple

Help someone out in a small way during your day. Hold a door, or help haul an item to their car (careful with hauling out of their car, this can easily be mistaken for stealing). Buy a coffee for someone in a low spot, send a smile to someone who looks like they are in need. You can change the course of someone's day, week, or even year with an act of random kindness and let's face it, helping others brings joy to our day that is tough to rival in any other way.

Something New

Experience something for the first time. Be an out-of-towner in your own city by exploring a new area. Take a new walking route, or if you are feeling really daring, take the back alley (daylight recommended). Find yourself plunging your hand into a cooler for a routine drink? Try out that ominous green juice that has been threatening you since the first cooler dive. It could be the best thing you have had all year. It is all too easy to slip into boring same-olds throughout the day, so bring back excitement by experiencing something new.

Practice Gratitude

Forget about the task list for 30 seconds of your day, and appreciate something you currently have in your life, whether it be your job, fancy stapler, or comfy couch. Appreciate the determined co-worker, passionate friend, or crazy mail person. Last but not least is your environment. Maybe it is a funky office space, beautiful park, or the endless sky. Time goes by all too quickly, and before you know it, the things we have worked so hard for can blend to nothing or disappear.

Kick it Old-School

Get rid of technology for two hours. No texts, emails or bright screens of any variety, just you and an abacus, or something like that. Enjoy the peace and quiet of no distractions or disruptions. It is a calming feeling when one realizes the world still rotates and the birds still chirp when electronics are not around.

Stepping Out of the Algorithm

Our lives are filled with decisions for us. Need to make it to the other side of town? Consult the oracle. Looking for a dinner spot? Consult the oracle. Booking a trip? Consult the oracle. The problem here is we completely lose sight of choice for ourselves and instead move towards choice of the masses and most attended spots.

The trap of the oracle: pawning decisions off on another to make data-driven decisions. The risk here is stepping further away from—and even losing—our choice.

Laugh

Have a plain old hearty laugh! Whether it's watching a funny movie, a phone call to a friend who lightens the mood, or busting out a new dry joke at work. Remember to stop taking yourself so seriously, and remember the power of a good old-fashioned laugh.

Relax

Certainly one of the hardest to do, yet one of the most valuable! Your body has emotional and physical batteries, and if you never rest, they never recharge. It is much easier to be happy on full batteries!

Make sure you keep track of these awesome little pieces of paper to show your progress and to reflect on the great times that were had. Throw it in a jar or box and it doubles as your next Pinterest pin! Grow rich and help others grow rich by spreading the heavy pockets method.

Happiness is a choice, and that choice starts with a pocket and a piece of paper!

Community

Friends and family are your secret weapon to a successful life.

A surprising study #LTESharvard

As we approach the final stage of this book, we find the most universally important ingredient to our happiness and life through the eyes of a smile, our relationships. I routinely ask people what brings them the largest smile in their day and I routinely hear back answers like the following: "When I walk through the door after a hard day's work and my daughter runs up and squeezes me." "Spending relaxing time together with my significant other." "What makes me the happiest is when the people around me are the happiest." Answers like these will not be far off from your answer to the simple question. What brings you the largest smile in your day? Stop and think about it.

A study is being performed at Harvard on adult development, spanning over 75 years. This study is tracking 724 men, asking them questions, performing brain scans, and conducting blood work all along the way to find indicators of their wellbeing. Two groups of men were studied. The first group started as sophomores in Harvard, and the second was a group of boys from Boston's poorest and most troubled neighbourhoods. The study has survived through four generations of researchers, and 60 of the original are still alive and participating in the study. What the study has uncovered is the quality of these men's lives is directly related to the quality of their relationships in life. Wealth, fame, and work ethic had nothing to do with it.

And it's true. Our money, fame, and hours spent behind a desk will not bring more smiles into our lives. All too often, though, this is the easy pill to accept in life, and let's face it, it is much more profitable for industries of all varieties to sell us this myth. There were three major findings of this study. The first was that social connections are very good for us and loneliness kills. The second was that the quality of our relationships reigns over the quantity. Lastly, physical pain can be controlled or magnified by the emotional satisfaction we have in our relationships.

We can be lonely in a crowd and lonely in a relationship, but it is the quality of your close relationships that matters. High conflict and no affection marriages are worse for our health than getting divorced. Those who were the most fulfilled in their relationships at midlife were the healthiest later in lives. Our emotional pain magnifies the physical. Good relationships protect our minds as well.

Quality reigns over quantity. We can have many people in our lives, but if these people are not positive and protecting there can be no personal value. We can be lonely in a crowd and lost in a relationship. In some cases, they can actually prove to be more harmful. It is much healthier for us to end relationships that are harmful to our emotions in the long run. In the short term, the easier solution will always be the most comforting, but the long-term effects can be disastrous.

Emotional pain magnifies physical pain, and emotional joy regulates pain to a normal level. When we have physical pain, which is very much associated with growing old, it was found that this pain was regulated to normal levels by good quality relationships. In some cases we can almost forget about physical pain when having a good laugh with a friend or when they surround us with positive energy. On the flip side, when we are experiencing tough emotional times our physical pain cranks up.

If happiness is so simple, though, then why are we not happier? Well, because of numerous reasons like our aversion to loss or the inability to cut negative people out of our lives. Another reason is that it's very hard to talk to people who are complete strangers to bolster our networks and bring in new people to our lives. And another is our general desire to only look for ways to take in a relationship, not give.

You Need More Nascar in Your Life
#LTESnascar

Nascar is one of the highest attended and subscribed-to sporting events in the world. They must be doing something right. What specific component of Nascar should we examine? Thousands of fans cheering us on? Jets flying over and parachute landings on big days? Stadiums built in our honor? You are probably thinking, "Well Calvin, that does sound pretty nice to me, but also completely insane." And it is. But here, I want to focus on Nascar's support crew.

The support crew gives the driver instant feedback on performance, has a diverse background to tune all pieces vital to performance, and the most important fact of all, they are all rooting for and supporting the success of the driver. Without a pit crew the driver would run out of gas, have a narrow view of the road ahead, lose traction, and surely finish far from their personal best. What would our lives look like if we had people to assist and provide a view from the outside on our actions and performance?

Writing this book was a daunting process when looking at it from afar. I had 1/6th as many words as I wanted and no idea what was involved in self-publishing. So I recruited the help of others. I recruited Melissa to put together a full plan of how to launch a book, Michelle to perform all of the edits, Sam to do the printing, and still at the time of writing these words, someone to create the cover! It was a large process, but when broken down into chunks it became very manageable. I needed to find people to help me figure this crazy thing out who were just as crazy as me. I wrote a few words a day. I sent out a request on Upwork for an editor. I looked on to fiverr to hire a cover artist. The most important part of all this was not just bringing any one person onto the team, but finding people who were also passionate about leading a life defined by smiles. These people were also in pursuit of life through the eyes of a smile.

You may not have desires to write a book, but you can still benefit from having a team rooting for you in life.

Look to your friends, and if you cannot find a team in your friends, start expanding your network to reach more like-minded individuals. Find groups of people who can complement each other. Perhaps you have a very craft-oriented passion or you enjoy fitness; perhaps the outdoors lies at the top of the list. Find a pit crew to take you to new heights in each category you address. Alone, you cannot take the journey to your personal best. It takes a team to go to new heights together. A team is a symbiotic relationship, whereas one-way relationships will do nothing but create toxicity in your life and leave you with the attitude that the world owes you more, and that you must be the unluckiest person in the world.

In my personal life, I have people I routinely work with on writing, spirituality, career, world exploration, and relationships. These people are all necessary to give me a good hard slap with a cold dish to smack me back into realism. And as a two way street, I hold others accountable to their success and happiness. These relationships will need to consist of reference points in our lives or where we want to get to. Candid conversations have to be had and maintained for this accountability to thrive. "Yes people" are not welcome here. You need people who know your goals and desires, who are willing to learn your personality and call out those lazy times when you abandon your goals. This is the difference between a nice and kind person. A nice person will do nothing but provide the emotional ease they think you need. They are there to protect you. In this process, however, they keep you away from much-needed progression. On the other hand, kind people hear you out, understand your ambitions, and help you improve with critical advice. Your pit crew should consist of kind people who are most interested in the well being and personal development of each other.

Why are we typically so resistant to having teams of people in our lives providing direction and input? One of the most harmful assumptions is that we are one-person all-stars who can change the world with no help along the way. Another aspect which really turns us off to these group mindset mentalities are schools. How fun were group projects when you were in school? The purpose of these groups was to assemble a group of people to seemingly shock you into the realism of the world outside, that some will float by with little to no provided value. We never got to choose the team, and memories of these times were typically, "Just hand me over the work and I will do it." Once we emerge from school, any group work is absolutely frowned at in follow up from the remembered pain. We have to remember that our experiences from the past aren't always precise indicators of experience in the future. We have the absolute advantage now of picking our teams based on who we see as helping the most and who we want to progress with in life. You may have a great friend who you spend a lot of time with, but this friend may not have the desire to improve at the same rate. Or perhaps you do not have any areas of life that you can help each other grow in. Unlike school, you do not have to choose these people to be in your pit crew.

We All Start at the Same Spot
#LTESchoices

We all start from the same spot in this world, but we all grow up having more and more choice of who we surround ourselves with. In the first phase of our lives, or up until we enter the career world, we are mostly surrounded by our immediate family and the friends we gain at grade school. Our mannerisms, language, and abilities mirror very closely that of this group in life. Off we then venture out of the house, and many times a new set of friends develops in post secondary or as moves occur. From here, we now spend most of our time with a new set of people and actively adopt traits very similar to them.

At any point in time, we have formed into the people we are because of those who surround us. This can be considered mirroring or even adapting by osmosis. Mirroring means adopting the traits of those around us, which happens naturally to us as human beings. If someone around us is on edge we grow on edge; if they are happy, we are naturally happy. Osmosis happens when we start to soak in the language and topics of interest that our close group contains. If this group talks about sports a lot, so will you. Politics, you have no choice. Pick the people who you admire and aspire to be like parts of them, and surround yourself with them! If only it were that easy...

My Mom Would Not Approve of Us Hanging Out #LTESmom

We are going to have people in our lives that our moms would not approve of. And as we go forward in life we learn our mothers are right most of the time, so what do we do with these people? We know they are not the most positive influence, but the social connection is too strong to just cut ties with them altogether. The typical advice people hand out when we run into troublesome time after troublesome time with them is to just remove them from our lives. I am not into routine advice, and this statement is too simplistic, just like, "Happiness is yours if you take it." Just removing someone from your life is not as easy as it sounds, and I am sure we can all relate to this. In extreme cases, this will be necessary, but only after going through a few steps.

I am creating change in my world. So often we hear comments from those closest to us in life that they are going to change, and so often they slip right back into their old routines. This is the case of broken record syndrome. By now you have in your mind an idea of how you are going to be creating a new path forward, and a major step here is to first tell people you are making this step. Those closest to us will most likely roll their eyes and dismiss the conversation as just another Sunday or Monday chat. This is where the change occurs. Instead of taking the massive leaps we desperately desire and failing within a matter of two weeks as per usual, we can take a different approach. We start by making small changes to our routine, progress starts to build over a period of time, and those around us start to notice change for once. If this change consists of less time with those who your mom does not approve of, and you have been clear to these people that you are making the changes to become a better version of yourself, they will begin to respect it. This time will be different if you just take small steps forward and have faith in your abilities. It is very important to only have those who lift you up in your support crew, not drag you down. Those who mom disapproves of can always still watch you race, they will just not have a say in the direction.

Finding New Support Crew Members
#LTESwolfPack

By now, it is no secret that our subconscious has to buy into our future better selves in order to find any progression. Buy-in from our subconscious is solidified through our faith in a better self tied up with a strong emotional connection. When looking at a great network from surface level, it is east to start dreaming of the number of CEOs you know or BMW owners or the people living in the same upscale neighbourhood as you. Now we know that that is just not true.

A quality network consists of a diverse set of people all sharing common passions and values. The emotional connection needed to build a substantial and quality network hit home with me this year when listening to Carly Cloge speak in Calgary of the challenging times she had been through as CEO of Ubooly. She was at a crossroads in her life after a hard-fought journey and nearing wits' end. She decided to pick up the phone and call her network to ask their advice regarding a serious crossroads. 100+ calls later, she had enough advice and input from her network to make a decision.

This floored me. The bonds in a network are only forged through multi-dimensional assistance, not one person. Think of all the issues you are having in your life right now, whether it's at home, the office, or anywhere else in your day-to-day. How would your life improve if you could make 100 phone calls to your minion tribe on these issues? How would the life of those in your network improve if they could call you for kind, personal advice on their life? How likely are you to assist those in your network in their time of need? This will be directly related to the help they are willing to give you. Think of the people now who are most willing to help you in life. How willing are you to help them? It is part of our human programming to want to help another person who has helped us in life. We experience the ups and downs of their lives, and we gain a very strong desire to help them, which is driven from the internal connection that ties your emotions to theirs. This is one of the most beautiful and troublesome parts of life. We are closely tied to those who are around us, but when we have no one, we let ourselves deteriorate. But it is not all dark. Remember back to "cheers to the future"—we have a beautiful life ahead of us that is completely in our control.

Like most of these items we are talking about, there are multiple sides and uses to take a look at. In sales, this routine is used very often: salespeople will offer someone a gesture of kindness before entering any conversation that could benefit them. This is done mostly with the offer of a coffee; think of this next time you walk into a car dealership. Were you offered a coffee or water in a compassionate way, and how did it help you to help them?

Now comes the question of how you meet new people who are interested in the same things as you. For starters, anywhere. A story that sticks in my mind of a very memorable people person actually comes from the mouth of another. Through conversation of the importance of connecting with people came the following story about Bob. Bob had an electric energy to him; he had the ability to connect two complete strangers. Bob made it his goal to meet and connect with a new person daily. Bob was known throughout the office building as the elevator guy. Never missing a beat, he would instantly introduce himself with a big smile to anyone new on the elevator. As the door opened on the next floor, he would introduce himself to the new person and then immediately introduce his new two friends to each other, creating another new connection! And of course he maintained relationships with all those people who he had met in the past. How fantastic it is to hear this story. Can you imagine the energy and complete laugh he would provide to you? Can you imagine getting on one floor, meeting a vibrant individual, and then having him pull the same thing to the person on the next floor and one-up it with introducing the two of you now?

Now Bob is of course an extreme, and we certainly should not shoot for this approach as a start. Instead, we want to think of the areas in our lives we would like to see the most improvement and target people who have the same interests and passions. Think about emotions for this one. What would it mean to have someone new in your life who loves (insert interest) here just as much as you do? How would your life improve? Perhaps you'd gain more opportunity to advance in your career, more ability to be active, or more opportunity to improve your knitting skills.

Now that we have identified the type of people we would like to meet and grow our network with, it is time to find the places to make this happen. Events in person are the logical start to most. Finding events can be a slog, however, so look to Facebook, Eventbrite and Google searches with keywords of your area you are looking to improve paired with "events." Let your emotions motivate you through this process. If you know that your life will get better by having more knitting-crazy people around, you must register and attend the event. Not all events will be a massive success, and you will most likely meet people who do not scratch an immediate itch in your life. However, you will also be surprised at the quality of people you meet when you walk through the door with this goal in mind. Also, you must help the other person with a problem in their life prior to expecting any value to come back to you. Through this interaction the relationship strengthens.

From family to work to passions and interests, these are all very important details to better understand the person sitting on the other side of the table. It is your goal to speak as little as possible at this point and to take as many notes on the shared interests and passions and potential coexist points for each other. Remember that you are boring and the other person is interesting. Think of how much you like to talk and hear your own voice; this is no different on the other side of the coin.

We all love to hear ourselves talk, especially about our interests, so you are in good shape.

We will now look at three very important questions to remember when talking with others to gain rapport fast. Rapport is most quickly achieved through shared interests and passions and emotional state transitions. More aptly, laugh and cry with the person on stuff you both love. Matching and sharing emotional states is what creates bonds. If you can both meet very serious tones and also share a laugh, you are in the good with this person. Keeping this in mind, the next three steps Location/Occasion, Careers/Passion and Long-term association have been adopted from David Snyder. First a little background to David as well as the conversational technique that this approach comes from. David Snyder has a long list of credentials and abilities throughout the spectrum of energy healing, martial arts, Neuro Linguistic Programming, hypnosis, and oriental medicine techniques. I highly recommend David's YouTube channel for a highly diverse selection of recorded training ranging throughout his fields. I was amidst an infamous YouTube exploration where I became quickly sidetracked after searching for who knows what. This is when I first came across his NLP work. For anyone who has not been exposed to NLP, it is a systems-based approach geared at instilling effective communication that was born in the 1970s. Many sales professionals have been through this training, and although popularity has slipped, it is still prominent in communications today. Listen to Tony Robbins? He trained with

John Grinder in the early days and still uses components of the methods in his teachings today. There are a few reads out there that will certainly be beneficial, but I believe that by simply watching a few hours of David Snyder online, you will be a good chunk of the way to reaping the main benefits of NLP.

When it comes down to it, we are all people at the core and if we dig deep enough, we find the root of communication. If we attain rapport at a deep enough level, we can have conversations with others on a level others would look at with complete confusion. This happens most often with mixed up words or phrasing: you or the other side completely messes up technically what is being said, but both sides understand. Have you ever completely understood someone without saying words? Or, by completing messing up words that onlookers would only shake their heads at, yet the person beside you had complete understanding? It was like they could complete your words for you sometimes without even talking. This is a deep state of rapport. No more awkward, "Hey...so...tell me something about yourself."

We tend to easily forget, and we also do not follow instructions very well. I have still botched many conversations; however, the number of quality and meaningful communication I have had recently is absolutely stunning. With a sincere approach to communication, people will open up to you about their values and passions within five minutes and confide in you like a friend of 25 years after an hour. The routine starts with a very simple conversation starter based around the location or the occasion. Nothing weird here, you are in the same place for a common interest or have ventured out (maybe at the will of friends).

Location/ Occasion

The action behind step one is to discover what brings a person to the event. Since you are both in the same place, you share a common bond. This is the opener and keeps things a little more exciting than "Hi." This works to start conversation, but it is much like trying to start a fire with wet sticks. What brings you to said event? Have you been here before?

Career/ Passions

Career is the gateway here as most people identify themselves with their careers. "What do you do?" stems a response that is career-based. You rarely ever hear, "I read, mountain bike, snowboard, ride horses." Although all these things are the strong connection points we are trying to reach, the career path is the best route. Find out where a person is now in their career, and strive to hear what has gotten them up to this point. Make sure to say something like, "I bet you are very proud of where you are" and congratulate the person. Now it is time to find out where they think they are going. Wrapping this all together...wow it sounds like you really have all this planned out. When did you know you wanted to be a caterpillar?

153

Long-term association

Taking it back now, when we recall events from the past we are simply playing a mock script of what actually happened. Ever wondered why some stories change so very often? Because our memory is never that good. When we remember back in these situations, we associate the person we are talking to with that memory and that feeling.

Going Deeper #LTESdeeper

Daniel Kahneman is a behavioural economist who, just like Dan Airely, questions the traditional assumptions made in economics. Daniel has dedicated much of his work to understanding our thought patterns and how they affect our decisions. He breaks this down into System 1 and system 2. System 1 addressing questions such as what is 3x2, what day is it this week, etc. System 2 is the part of us that gets the joy of answering questions like 325*2.5 or, what was your third favorite part of today.

Our ability to create new relationships and bolster old ones relies heavily on our conversational skills. Our wolf packs, tribes, and minion herds will never grow at a substantial rate using the daily canned and dead-end conversation starters like "How are you doing today? What's going on? How was your evening?" Questions like these inspire responses such as "Good. Not much. Alright." These conversations provide little value other than filling awkward space between two people. To improve our relationships we need to start taking conversations into much deeper, and more meaningful places. The good news is that we can set the bar low, leaving us with heaps of room to improve. Here are a few more starters:

"What are you looking forward to today?"

Used best at the start of the day, this is a great way to assist people into the hours ahead. The day can seem very, very long, especially prior to the first cup of coffee. By asking about the most exciting part of the day, we transport that person right into their upcoming highlight reel. It is like having your cake and eating it too.

"What has been the highlight of your day?"

The day is coming to end, and minds are worn down from the many challenges faced. It is time to rewind the clock and celebrate the day with a dedication to the best experience. With a slight modification for the morning, this is a great way to shed the dread of the day ahead. You can also ask, "What was the highlight of your night?"

"Tell me about ___?"

The last piece of the puzzle is to add memory to conversation. Remember your conversations from the day before and follow up on them. Memory is the most important building block of any relationship. In order to gain the admiration of the person on the other side of the conversation, we need to show them we actually listen. This is the glue to any relationship.

Your choice of words and tone inspire emotion. It is natural for us to adopt the demeanor of the person on the other side of the conversation, so be mindful of your tone and pace. If you speak with hesitation, the person on the other side of the

156

conversation will match it. If you speak in a rush this will translate across to the other person, indicating shortness of time. We also have the ability to steer the conversation in emotional directions. For example, the sentences above have been chosen carefully to inspire positive emotion. What are you looking forward to? What has been the highlight of your day? Both of these steer the conversation directly into a positive light.

Prior to System 2 conversation, it was shooting arrows into the dark with no real feedback on effectiveness. Making System 2 conversation into a game gives you the distinct advantage of connecting deeply with others. This game also keeps the focus on what you can do in conversation. Move through the 3 steps to rapport and you should consider your conversation a success. We no longer focus on the external validation that consists of the response we get from another. This attitude is very much the mindset of high-performing teams, as well. You can still have a personal best game if you lose on the scoreboard. In reverse, the scoreboard can show a win and the game was a complete under performance of peak quality. This personal best inward out philosophy was adapted by John Wooden over his famed career highlighted by 10 NCAA championships in 12 years. Feedback in the form of validation from the outside in, like a scoreboard, will only create confusion internally. I played my best but still lost, I had a great conversation and touched all the right points and the person would not give me the time of day for a follow up.

Having someone reject a conversation or dismiss the content of the conversation is not always an indicator of quality, so it should be not be the indicator of success, either. Conversational success should be matched by achieving a deeper level of conversation and in learning more about the person on the other side of your words. If you find out what makes a person unique, what they are passionate about, and where they are going, you have found success.

WTF #LTESwtf

With any type of communication, we will find barriers that will pop up from time to time. Have you ever gotten the look, or perhaps even the comment of "WTF are you talking about?" when trying to explain a new project, idea, or plan? What a task it proves to be when we are so deeply involved in the concepts and ideas that we cannot remove ourselves far enough to provide a simple and understandable overview to an outsider. Next time you get this face, or comment, dissect WTF into three components to help explain the thought at hand. Use W as the "why": why you are doing what you are doing. Use T for the technicalities, otherwise known as the differentiators, or what makes this thought unique and special. Follow that up with F for the future. What strategic planning lies ahead?

W (Why)

At the end of the why, the person on the other side should understand the internal motivation behind the thought (not money or fame as these are both external motivators). Why you are doing something stems from meaning, the motivation and desires from within. Without this, the idea will be prone to inconsistent messaging and not staying true to a purpose, likely sending the listener the in the direction of, "This goes completely against everything discussed recently."

T (Technicalities)

After hearing the technicalities, the person listening to you should be able to identify the components of your thought that make it so special. What are you doing differently than everyone else? What sets you apart from the pack? Without the technicalities, your speech will blend with many others out there, sending the listener into wondering what's for dinner instead of focusing on you.

F (Future)

What does the future of the thought look like? This is the strategic planning portion where you wrap up the thought with what the future has to hold, proving that the idea is no dead end. Establish a vision to the thought and gain further connection and insight by laying the path ahead. Without this step, speculation can arise, and people will wonder if your idea has been fully thought out.

Next time you get the WTF sense, use this as a reminder to frame ideas with. Why – the story up until today. Technicalities – unique details that set this idea apart. Future – the vision going forward. Using the WTF method, listeners on the other end of the conversation will quickly be placed into context of even the most complicated ideas.

I recently witnessed this five minute plus dispute with two co-workers at a McDonalds (I can be a sucker for McMuffins) at a point of high stress after a large order arrived. The person was not there yet to pick up the large order, but the time must have been ticking until their arrival. In the meantime, the line at the till was doing nothing but growing with the influx of customers and their small orders.

Person A – Why aren't you helping me out? I am completely overloaded, and I asked you to help five minutes ago.

Person B – No you didn't. You said stay at the till.

Person A – Why would I say that? I am completely over-loaded!

Person B – No, I heard you say stay at the till.

Person A – No I didn't, etc.

From the outside it appeared the one person operated calmly whereas the other operated in high stress mode. Each had the facts straight in their heads and neither was going to back down. Both were in states of overload, one at the till and one preparing food. In the eyes of Person A, they were doing all the hard and necessary work while the other person was at the till continuing to pile workload on them. In the eyes of Person B, it was very important to keep the new customers satisfied, and Person A was overreacting. With only a few simple adjustments to serve the customers that were actually there, the problem decreased in magnitude. Both were arguably operating as they should have in their roles and they were equally important, so who was right with the facts?

Now from an expert opinion, it may be very clear that person A or B was wrong; however, the world is not as cut and dried as numbers may dictate. When emotions are involved, the world takes a slant of irrationality. Coming back to Dan Ariely, if the world was cut and dried by the numbers, then traditional economics would rule, and no economic problems would be present in this world. Every decision we made would be in our best rational interests. But this is not the case. We know the salad is the best option for us on a diet, but as hunger starts to encroach, we easily rationalize the need of a burger. Now, let's review this situation from both sides to try and paint a new picture instead of a dead ended, resentment-loaded order of 16 McDonald's oatmeals.

Person B Steps into Person A's Shoes

Person A – Why aren't you helping me out? I am completely overloaded, and I asked you to help five minutes ago.

Person B – I thought you said stay at the till. How are you doing back there?

Person A – I am feeling completely overloaded with this order, and I cannot keep up with all the new people coming in.

Person B – Okay, I absolutely see you are overloaded, and these new orders are not helping. The big order is not here yet, so let's get some of these people their orders who have been waiting. I will help you out.

Person A – Oh, okay, thanks for your help. That is a great idea. I will start working on the first few orders of the people waiting, so please help me get this large order out of the way.

Person A Steps into Person B's Shoes

Person A – Why aren't you helping me out? I am completely overloaded, and I asked you to help five minutes ago.

Person B – No you didn't. You said stay at the till.

Person A – Oh, I could have sworn I asked you. Would you be able to help me out with this large order?

Person B – There is a really large line up of people coming in, and I think we should serve them first since they are actually here.

Person A – Okay, I see there are quite a few people waiting. I think it would be great to help some of them out. Would you be able to help me with the first four people in line?

These two perspectives involve stepping into the shoes of another at times of high stress. The conversation transforms from one-way dictation being fired back and forth using perceived facts from only one pair of shoes at a time, to a two-way conversation of bridged understanding. This seems so easy in writing or from the outside looking in. But solving issues this way, with facts, doesn't work because facts are validated as true in our own minds.

Whether it is climate change, dirty oil, or political alignment, we have all seen the facts and how no argument is ever solved this way. If the argument/conversation happens to be between two completely rational humans or between two computers then we have our formula to success. Life will be an isolated and unhappy mess leading with nothing but facts. But reaching for a deeper level of understanding to another's viewpoint will reduce stress, reduce feelings that the world is against you, and increase the quality of relationships in your life. There is nothing more we hate to hear than we are wrong, and nothing more we love to hear that we are right. By telling the other person you see their viewpoint and recycling their words, it tells them we are listening.

Meaningful and understood conversations occur when WTF1 is added to WTF2. Typical and very confused surface-level conversation occurs when F1 clashes with F2. In this scenario, neither side is understood in regards to where their opinion comes from or the current tools at disposal to make things happen.

Your Message #LTESyou

The most efficient way to find others who are like you is to make sure you know what you stand for and can communicate it. By having a clear and consistent message for others to see, it becomes much easier for people to gravitate towards you. Think of the people who you gravitate to most in life. How often do these people change their minds on what they stand for? Very rarely. As humans our brains consistently search for patterns, and we do not like changing messages as it brings in uncertainty to our lives. Do you know someone who is always flip-flopping with their message? How do you feel about them?

Our message first starts with how we carry ourselves. When we walk down the street, we start first with the posture we hold. When entering a room or conversation for the first time, we are drawn to those who match our own body language. From here, conversation dominates. If you have similar physical states to another, it will not matter if your values and opinions are in stark contrast. You will not gravitate towards each other more than the initial match on physiology. It is just like the watering hole at work, cliques form and like species gather together. From here speech dominates. From afar it can seem like you have a lot in common with someone. Strong posture and eye contact is different than lesser posture and weaker eye contact. I am not going to connect very strongly with you and your journey if you do not speak with passion, or if you say your favorite color is red one day and blue the next. Great Calvin, how do I tell my story? Start with the past. It shapes who we are now, not defines—there is a difference here. Now what are you doing today, and what skills make that special? Where are you going? Sure, the direct tasks may not be clear, but a defined mission is required.

Pleasing the entire world sounds great, but at the same time, it creates a very confusing message that is nearly impossible to be a part of.

Let's take a look at a few of the biggest crowd based sites in the world, YouTube and Facebook. The most subscribed to individual on these platforms is Cristiano Ronaldo. Cristiano Ronaldo stands as the face of soccer.

Smosh is the highest subscribed to channel on Youtube at this time and have occupied the top spot over much of the past decade. Smosh is a duo that started off with lip-syncing game theme songs such as Power Rangers, Mortal Kombat, and Pokémon. Their breakthrough into a massive following came after the Pokémon video release. The lip-synced song was consistent to their message of game theme songs and took them to over 24 million views before being taken down. They have stayed consistent to their initial videos with continuing game and comedy content.

Online Networking #LTESipfriends

Now comes the largest opportunity we have to meet people today, online.

Traps to the networking mindset and traps to abandoning social media are all the same. If you want to improve your life, hard reflection is needed. Prior to this book launch, who was in my network at that point in life was not in line with who I was; it created internal struggles with my values and my beliefs. No wonder I abandoned Facebook, I would be crazy to put myself through the emotional strain everyday of reading posts that troubled me. Instead, surround yourself with people who inspire you, people who give you ideas, and people you can help out and who are willing to help. No different than in your personal face to face life, if someone is a constant drain on you these people should be distanced. Easier said than done, now isn't it.

Start with conversations of BRS. Maybe the person does not know they are afflicted. Have serious, deep conversations and be true to your stance. If you are telling a friend their behaviour impacts you negatively and then you go right around and display behaviour that impacts them negatively, the relationship won't work well. My return to Facebook and my trust in other social platforms was driven directly from a life-changing experience on LinkedIn. I built a network from ground zero that existed of little to no negative acquaintance influence from before. The basis of this build was based on shared career goals and insights. This was a truly value-based network. The values I had matched the values of others through a pre-screening process. Social media is great. You get to be a fly on the wall before joining the conversation and before joining networks. It is not like you are walking down the grocery store and have to meet everyone you encounter just to see if you have shared interests. If this was the case, we would all walk around with big signs strapped to us or even perhaps shirts like billboards. Passions on the back, business in the front, and maybe even different colors for personalities. With the Internet we have this luxury in the form of "creeping," or in a much better term, informing ourselves.

Going with the theme of individuality, your goal is to be the same person in all places of your life. Therefore, it is a real shame to explain yourself by only using skills that you have collected at work. These skills are common and on the exact same level as connecting with people on similar cars or neighbourhoods. You need to have your values and passions shine through in profiles; this is how people are truly attracted to you.

Building a voice is the most important aspect to any networking. Online your voice spreads and in a room you must use your voice and opinion to gain rapport with those who are there. Building voice is done through interactions. Whether it be reposting comment, flagging, commenting or original content, this is a very important step. If you are silent and in the corner there will be next to nothing to judge a person on.

Clicking Connect #LTESlinkedin

This section is dedicated to LinkedIn, as it has been where I have spent the most time online. However, the approach stays the same across all networking whether it be on or offline. It is all about finding others who share the same interests and then working together to add value to each other's lives. The more people you know and assist, the fewer problems you will have in life. One of the largest hurdles we face is connecting with people, especially in the online world. It is generally seen as creepy connecting with someone you do not know. Creepy pops up when we see no reason to connect other than trying to make social media a dating platform or way to scope on the neighbours without having to walk to the window. The new trigger you are going to use for connecting with someone else will be when you catch yourself thinking, "Hmmm interesting" or "Wow, that is cool." As a general rule of thumb if you are interested in the person you should tell them and connect.

Hover over the blue connect box, displace the doubt, and drive the left mouse button down. Expand your business network globally. Create new opportunities. Find your desired mentors.

Global Networking

Seek and connect with individuals across the world who share your passion. A common bond of vocation and desire to assist others is all you will need to grow your network. How do you find people to connect with? Detailed filters will allow you to search based on multiple parameters, allowing for highly customized searches. Once your network starts building you will quickly receive news from others in your network on their interests. This is a great way to build your network. Surround yourself with those who interest you and those who bring fresh perspectives to your day. Social media is now the on-demand news that is customized to you. From Canada, to Australia, to China, expand your network globally.

Opportunities

With the current economic situation we are in, I am sure you have noticed a surge in posts and group activity. For most individuals it takes a nudge like losing a job to push their personal development. When posting or commenting on a peer's question, you are building value in yourself. With every post and question answered, you are establishing your passion and spreading your name. LinkedIn is your dynamic resume available to the world, as your experience increases, update your profile. New followers and invitations to connect will start rolling in, and you will surely have new opportunities arise which never before existed.

Mentorship

In your line of work, who are the stars? They are the individuals pushing the forefront of innovation and those who have taken your line of work to where it is now. Chances are very good you can find them on LinkedIn and connect. Set a flag and follow all of their actions in the form of posts. Send a personalized message, and extend your virtual hand for a greeting. I am lucky enough, in my chosen line of work, to have numerous stars that continually follow groups and provide valuable insight to those seeking knowledge. At the same time, you can be ensured incorrect or inaccurate information will be identified and corrected in a timely fashion. Just as we rely on group input to drive Google Maps and Wikipedia, integrity is ensured by the masses on LinkedIn.

Having uncertainties?

What if they don't accept? Do I look creepy by adding someone I have never met before? These questions, and more, are likely to surge through your head alongside a mounting heartbeat as the uncertainties build. Like any social interaction in person, you will have greetings that go nowhere, and those that continue on past first greetings. If a request goes nowhere, do not take it personally. We all lead busy lives, and an un-returned request can stem from multiple possibilities outside of our influence. That being said, LinkedIn connections are much more likely to blossom when a personalized, meaningful message is created. For example, a simple click of the connect button generates the canned response:

"I'd like to add you to my professional network on LinkedIn."

Placing more effort into the request, the result can look like the following:

Hi Judith, I couldn't agree more with your latest publish on XYZ, it would be a pleasure to connect and share thoughts in the future,

Calvin.

Placing yourself on the other side of the request now, which are you more likely to accept in your network? Place the uncertainties behind you, and venture out in pursuit of meaningful connections.

Click Connect

As we progress through the years, the world around us is in constant evolution. Embrace the evolution of business networking and click that connect button. If you never say hello, you will never know.

Do I Know You? #LTESmeeting

"Wow. You look familiar, where do I know you from? Joan's friend?"

"Nope."

"Hmm okay. Do you work at the store on the corner of Ninth?"

"Nope."

"Okay one last guess, you must live in Tower Nine!"

"No, sorry."

Has it ever popped to mind that you may know someone from the online world? These expansive networks of friends, colleagues and acquaintances sharing common interests all bombard us with information throughout the day.

Online Interaction and Image

In public a familiar face is quickly spotted from the multitude of images associated with nearly all online interactions. Like or dislike, posts and shared articles combine to build patterns, giving you an insight into a person's passions and tendencies, much like conversation. Through visual recognition and the insights from online interaction, you can know people very well prior to meeting them. Being aware of your online image is a must; just as you would carry yourself in a public setting, know that many others have their eyes on your actions across all platforms. It is possible and more likely everyday that you will know someone online prior to meeting in person these days.

Getting Acquainted

Use online network connections to your advantage, and get to know individuals prior to meeting them. Add products like Rapportive to your Gmail to gain an overview of that person's LinkedIn profile next to any incoming or outgoing email. Add the Charlie app to have a detailed report pulled from the Internet, Facebook and Twitter for all attendants of your upcoming meetings. Need insight on an individual? Send Charlie on a solo mission and watch the information roll in, enhancing the quality of your interaction. You are currently on the eHarmony of the business world. LinkedIn matches you to potential contacts on many common levels, and you should take it no differently than a business introduction from a friend and make the connection.

Creepy or informed?

I choose informed. These days information is strewn across the Internet. By increasing your online exposure and searching out new meaningful connections, a whole new realm of interactions will invigorate your day to day.

"Wow, you look familiar, LinkedIn right?"

"Hey, yes you bet. I really enjoy your weekly posts for reasons A, B, and C, it is great to meet you."

Life is all about finding those who are your type of crazy to celebrate and solve problems with.

Conclusion

Success is defined by the quality and quantity of smiles you were able to achieve over a lifetime.

The End #LTESwrap

When we dedicate ourselves to life through the eyes of a smile, we look to the present and to the future. This life is focused on what you can do every single day to increase the quality and quantity of smiles over a lifetime, which for us is the ultimate goal. For most of us reading this book, we have been statistically grouped into the least happy times of our lives. We can accredit this to our saved moments when we grew up into close-minded adults, expecting a stork to drop off a beautiful life on our doorstep at any time. We set into a routine out of school that sets us up for a nice cozy life of 40 hours a week or more dedicated to a craft we more or less fell into. What are the chances you picked what is right for you upon entering the workforce? Existential Sundays set in and the thoughts started to arise of what meaning is in my life? What is my purpose in life? Birds fly past and again, no stork drops off our calling and life becomes even more confusing.

We start dreaming of this thing everyone talks about and seems to have called their passions. We see social media statuses of others claiming to have found their passion, and this simply adds to the self-doubt that is quickly growing like a weed in a garden. As we start experimenting with all the other things people tell us we should be doing in life, our self-identity starts to become mis-formed. Questions arise of who we should be at this moment. Whether it be at work, in our relationships, or in diverse friend groups, it becomes all too confusing who we should be, and at times we lose who we are. Doors open in our lives and we learn to cordially close them, just like polite Canadians, instead of daring to open them further and walk through them. Hope begins to rule our lives, and much like the lottery, we hope one day that it will all be better and that with time will come a happier life. We learn that our mind is a place that has our best interests at heart, but like an overprotective parent, it needs to step out of the way more often than step in.

The massive leaps of faith we hold ourselves accountable to work well for the perfect version of ourselves, but we know that is nothing but smoke and mirrors in our real world. We say over and over we would like to make changes and then conveniently forget about them. Our friends and family think oh, not again, I wonder how long this attempt at change will last before failing again. Looking backwards into our life we consciously find the notches which make us into a broken record and we have our first high value improvements to focus on. This is a chapter of surprise for our closest family and friends who have witnessed us try to change before, only this time we have a dear friend with us. In creeps our friend faith, who has never died, and we have a mental partner in our journey, a partner that refuses to give up. When we find our faith in a better life we must hold onto it, as it will be the driving force to propel us forward through the confusing times. The celebration starts now as our focus shifts to creating the wonderful life we will leave behind. We take a look at what we want to be remembered for in life through the eyes of a smile, we imagine the type of people we have yet to meet and the places we have yet to visit. This life is pivoted around small actions we can take every single day, not getting caught up in the details we have no say in. We look into the past with the awareness that we cannot change it, and instead, we choose to learn from it.

Here is where we pinpoint recurring features in our life that have seemed like a good idea at the time but instead have only proven to be mirages in the desert. Looking to others, we can start to model our future based off of their past success, taking things with a grain of salt along the way, keeping cautious not to be poisoned by advice that has the ability to harm us as much as help. Shedding the misconception that we can only learn from those who are in a perceived higher position, we open a door that is ripe for opportunity and learning from all in life. Focus will naturally need to shift from our worries to the great things we have the opportunity to create each and everyday. Progression is highlighted as paramount to our life, and we must take a hard look at where we have stalled out and take small steps to make the change we need to feel fulfilled and happy. If we ever stop we grow stale, as does the quantity and quality of smiles in our life. Conscious actions towards the end vision of our better self take form through squared exercises to build our self-worth and confidence.

When we are presented with a game-like layout in our lives, we are much more likely to actively pursue our end game with ambition and energy. With small daily reminders stuffed into our pockets, we have no choice other than to lift ourselves up as well as the others around us as we complete these daily actions. The final piece to our puzzle is after we set our daily actions, it is about the people we share this wonderful life with. Our current pit crew is likely quite lacking of substantial feedback and partners in life progression. Searching out, we need to look to interpersonal interactions that have been awkward and confusing in the past. Social media starts to take on a new light, and we don't use it anymore just to keep in contact with National Geographic-like displays of mating dances. Now we start to look at these platforms as a means of searching worldwide for inspiration and improvement.

Within these pages we do not have the perfect path forward; however, we have learned the perfect path is one that must be forgotten. The path we must dedicate ourselves to is one where we keep our faith on the ultimate goal in life.

Thank you for being a part of this movement dedicated to creating your life through the eyes of a smile.

Contact me at Calvin@happful.com with your successes, failures, and plain and simple questions about life whenever they come up.

Most Impactful Reads (In order read)
#LTESreads

The Game - Neil Strauss

This book has a clear target audience of young males who are entranced with fear while being around the opposite sex. This book teaches valuable connection skills and concepts while teaching life lessons on the value of finding the one person to spend life with. This was the first book I ever picked up that taught me skills and built my confidence directly from using concepts taught within.

Lessons - Fighting fear in interactions. Being able to open conversation with a stranger. Short term pleasures (bad happiness carbs) leave large holes in our long term happiness and fulfillment.

How to Win Friends and Influence People –

Dale Carnegie

This book really does not need an introduction, as it is one of the longest living classics at the top of most people's lists. Dale introduces and solidifies the understanding of how people interact and think. Still living on today, many salespeople and managers from around the world have the opportunity to be a part of this training to hone their ability to understand others.

Lessons – The value in interacting with others. Speaking and self-confidence.

Wooden On Leadership - John Wooden

From the legendary UCLA basketball coach who won 10 NCAA championships in a span of 12 years comes a book on so much more than the title alludes to. At the core of this book lies advice for achieving personal best as defined from the inside out, not the outside in. Validation from news, scoreboards or fans does not exist in the world of Wooden. Personal best is defined from the hard work demonstrated every single day in creating a better self.

Lessons – You can play the best game of your life and still lose on the clock. It takes a team to get anything done; no one should ever be singled out in a team.

Predictably Irrational - Dan Ariely

We do not think in terms of what will be the best for us. A dollar is not always worth a dollar depending on the situation we are in or the feeling that we have. Dan covers all aspects of life from work to relationships to pastimes, giving us a perspective on why we make the decisions we do.

Lessons – We suck at making decisions, but we can improve.

Thinking for a Change - Daniel Kahneman

System 1 is the fast automatic response that we rely on most of the day to guide us through life. System 1 has very many holes in it that leave us coming up over and over again with misguided steps forward. System 2 is much harder to activate, but when we do access it our ability to make better life decisions is amplified.

Lessons – Use atypical questions to force people to think deeply. Ask yourself atypical questions to improve your life.

It's Time to Sell - Chris Spurvey

Meant for the sales professional but written from core concepts of human function, Chris leads us down a path of personal best and self development which contains a very strong emotional connection. Chris is a Canadian eh and always willing to talk to anyone, I recommend you visit him on LinkedIn and tell him I sent you.

Lessons – Success runs deeper than title or money. Hunger is one of the most valuable driving forces in life. Hunger for a better life, especially when your life impacts others.